Teaching Children to Love Themselves

a handbook for parents and teachers of young children

Michael E. Knight
Terry Lynne Graham
Susan Robichaud Miksza
Rose A. Juliano
Pamela G. Tonnies

A SPECTRUM BOOK

PRENTICE-HALL, INC., Englewood Cliffs, N.J. 07632

Library of Congress Cataloging in Publication Data
Teaching children to love themselves.

   (A Spectrum Book)
   Bibliography: p.
   Includes index.
   1. Classroom management. 2. Self-respect—
Study and teaching. 3. Activity programs
in education.   I. Knight, Michael E.
LB3013.T39   372.11,02   81-11989
                                  AACR2

0-13-891671-3 {PBK}

0-13-891689-6

This Spectrum Book is available to businesses and organizations
at a special discount when ordered in large quantities. For information,
contact Prentice-Hall, Inc., General Book Marketing,
Special Sales Division, Englewood Cliffs, N.J. 07632

10 9 8 7 6 5 4 3 2 1

Printed in the United States of America

Editorial production/supervision and interior design
by Cyndy Lyle Rymer
Manufacturing buyer: Cathie Lenard
Cover design by Velthaus and King
All original poetry by Terry Lynne Graham unless otherwise indicated.
Illustrations by or adapted from originals by Kim Mitter.

Prentice-Hall International Inc., *London*
Prentice-Hall of Australia Pty. Limited, *Sydney*
Prentice-Hall of Canada, Ltd., *Toronto*
Prentice-Hall of India Private Limited, *New Delhi*
Prentice-Hall of Japan, Inc., *Tokyo*
Prentice-Hall of Southeast Asia Pte. Ltd., *Singapore*
Whitehall Books Limited, *Wellington, New Zealand*

Contents

iii

Preface

Teaching Children to Love Themselves provides classroom teachers and parents with a wide variety of activities that have been used to develop positive self-concepts and to promote the academic achievement of young children. The procedures and materials presented involve the children actively in their own education. Specific activities are designed to reach children from the preschool level through later elementary years and are easily adapted for any grade level.

The classroom management guide provides ready-to-use suggestions for creating a positive learning environment. Teachers will find new ideas and direction for setting up a classroom that enhances the child's self-image.

The parent pages are designed to encourage development of the self-concept through a unified approach—home and school working together. The activities encourage parents to be actively involved in their child's learning as well as contributing to the child's positive self-concept.

The reader will find that it is necessary to provide children with activities to grow continuously throughout the year. These needs are met by a chapter designated specifically for this purpose.

The self-concept activities represent the basic curriculum areas: language arts, the creative arts, science, and math. This enables the teacher to incorporate self-image growth in his or her daily routine and academic currriculum.

The learning situations presented here have all been successfully used by classroom teachers in diverse economic and social settings. Practical experience stimulated the creation and subsequent modification of these situations. The limited availability of learning materials in the area of self-concept led to the development of practical, easy-to-use ideas and experience.

All children should feel that they are special. We hope, through the use of this book, that you will give your children that special feeling, and you'll find that you'll feel special too!

Teaching Children
to Love
Themselves

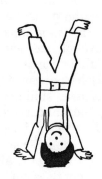

1

Introduction

Self-concept refers to an individual's perception of self in terms of ability, value, worth, and limitations. From the earliest years of childhood our perceived self becomes the starting point for the learning and experiences that form the person we become. Children have collected enough reflections of themselves to form estimations of their worth at a very young age. These reflections come from experiences encountered through social interactions with parents, teachers, siblings, relatives and peers and are constantly modified by these experiences. A child who is convinced by age four that he is a failure will have little motivation to achieve.

The self-concept is a human attribute that must be achieved. It is not a given trait. There has been general agreement that self-concept does not exist at birth. Its development begins soon after birth and continues throughout life. However, one's self-concept is not developed in isolation from other factors in a child's life. Each part influences every other part. That's why there is a need for the development of a school program that emphasizes the enhancement of the self-concept through the development of skills and abilities that a child possesses.

An individual develops a positive self-concept by continual evidence of his adequacy, especially during early childhood and in the primary grades. Since formal schooling occupies this latter period, we regard continual evidence of success or failure in school as likely to have major effects on the individual's self-concept.

Some Definitions of Self-Concept

There are many definitions of self-concept. Which of the following statements fit your understanding of self concept?

_____ 1. The self-concept refers to a sum total of all of the characteristics people attribute to themselves, and the positive and negative values they assign to these characteristics.

_____ 2. Self-concept involves feedback given by the significant others in a child's life.

_____ 3. It is the children's inner world—a composite of their thoughts and feelings, strivings and hopes, fears and fantasies, their view of what they are, what they have been, what they might become, and their attitudes pertaining to their worth.

_____ 4. Children who assert themselves are taking an important step in the development of their selves.

2

___ 5. There are perceived and real appraisals by significant others in the child's life.

___ 6. When children are able to compare themselves with their peers and are able to compete with them, they are also taking steps toward the formation of their self-concept.

___ 7. Children who develop strong relationships with their peers have good feelings about themselves.

___ 8. A child who is willing to take risks is usually a child with a positive self-concept.

___ 9. Children who have positive attitudes towards others have positive attitudes toward themselves.

___ 10. The way children respond to failure frequently provides a clear picture of their self-concept.

___ 11. A child has *many* self-concepts.

___ 12. Self-concepts are changing continuously.

Each of these statements is true concerning self-concept. (Rogers, 1951; Jersild, 1960; Sullivan, 1959; Briggs, 1970; Combs and Snygg, 1949; and Adler, 1935.)

Even though there are several definitions of self-concept, there is agreement among the descriptions of it. The self-concept is viewed as the way an individual perceives himself and his behavior, and is strongly influenced by the way others perceive him. The family gives the child his first basis for understanding the world and also provides the raw material from which self and personality are formed. The anxiety a child first experiences as an infant continues to have an effect on his behavior throughout his life.

EFFECTS OF A POSITIVE OR NEGATIVE SELF-CONCEPT

A child who is accepted, approved of, respected, and liked for himself or herself is better able to acquire an attitude of self-acceptance and respect. If the significant people in the life of a child belittle or reject him, his self-concept is likely to become unfavorable. These significant people include parents, teachers, siblings, peers, and others who influence the child's experiences. They help the child develop attitudes relating to his self, his social self, and his cognitive self.

Children who see themselves as unliked, unwanted, unaccepted, and unable to perform, frequently become maladjusted and are frustrated in society. Children with positive views are better adjusted and more able to adapt to different social settings. A fundamentally positive self-concept gives the child a basic strength for dealing with situations in life.

Self-concept is felt to be a directing force in all behavior. The idea that a person's self-concept influences his behavior has long been a part of American psychological thought, and it's been emphasized that a person's beliefs about himself will influence his decisions and actions.

INFLUENCES ON THE DEVELOPMENT OF SELF-CONCEPT

Significant others, family, teachers, peers, are crucial in a child's development of self-concept. How he perceives others feel about him and his accomplishments helps determine how he, in turn, will feel about himself.

Social and economic class, racial and ethnic background, and birth order are some of the factors from which our selves are formed. Each individual then integrates this raw material of heredity and experience in a unique manner, for himself.

Self-concept originates from four major sources: (1) impressions received from significant others; (2) the child's own personal experiences; (3) the child's own ability to set realistic goals for himself; and (4) the child's ability to judge himself by his own standards. Self-concept develops out of interpersonal relationships, and it strives for consistency. Each child has a basic need for a positive regard from both himself and others.

TEACHER'S INFLUENCE ON THE CHILD'S SELF-IMAGE

The teacher is in control of many aspects of learning which have a direct impact upon the child's perception of himself. Many children are afraid to confront new learning situations and feel that they are

4

unworthy. The teacher can help to change these negative feelings by promoting warm and accepting relations and eliminating anxiety. The teacher's daily activities and plans, the emotional climate that is set, and the teacher's control of the flow of interaction, and even the language used by the teacher have a great impact on self-image.

When a child feels he is accepted by his teacher and his peers, he is able to accept himself as a valued and worthy person. Teachers need to offer sincere praise and constructive criticism so that children will gain confidence in their own abilities. Teachers also need to provide a setting where children have opportunities to work with one another, to get to know one another, and to be friends. When children move freely within the classroom, they learn to appreciate the abilities of others and recognize differences in character and talents. In an enhancing environment, a child learns to view differences as positive attributes rather than viewing differences as a means to isolate or separate.

Teachers need to be aware of each child's developmental level and their personal backgrounds. The teacher should not base expectations of the child on testing data and theoretical norms. When this is done, many children quickly sense that their efforts are disappointing to the teacher. Studies show that children achieve according to the judgment of the teacher. The feelings of the teacher become a self-fulfilling prophecy. The teacher must get to know and understand the child and the child's many self-concepts in order to ascertain the child's learning style. A teacher must then select appropriate materials and activities that will enable the child to succeed and learn in the style best suited to him. If the child succeeds in school and has good feelings about himself, this will lead to continuing development of a positive self-concept. However, success in school has a broader definition than simply attaining good grades in the academic areas. Consideration must be given to the social and emotional needs of the child. Opportunities for cooperative work and sharing activities should be an integral part of the daily program.

The teacher's choice of incentives and motivation styles influences the self-concept of the child. Social incentives should offer opportunities for prestige and group support for all children.

Humiliation, criticism, and sarcasm have a devastating effect on the self-concept and should not be used.

How the teacher uses authority may support or hinder the development of a positive self-concept. Children should be allowed to participate in making the rules. A child feels good about himself when he is given the chance to make a choice regarding his own behavior and environment. Children who feel they are in control of their lives take more responsibility for their actions, seek challenges, and bounce back more readily from failure.

The teacher's method of grouping can also affect self-concept. Children soon sense their worth in strict systems of grouping and may begin to feel inferior. The labeling of these groups often becomes another self-fulfilling prophecy. When a variety of groupings, such as interest, specific teaching needs, or a task to be accomplished, is used, each child can appraise himself in different settings. He can recognize his strengths and limitations and those of others.

School, alone, cannot make up for deficits that may stem from a family's approach to child-rearing. It is not supposed to be what psychiatrists call a "therapeutic environment" designed to heal the emotionally disturbed. Nonetheless, what teachers do, or fail to do, inevitably enhances a child's sense of self or chips away at it. It should be remembered that what any of us is able to accomplish depends in no small measure on our sense of self, on a belief that we can succeed. We all tend to do what we expect of ourselves, and, that, in turn, is largely derived from what others expect of us.

The "I think I can" approach from the classic picture book, *The Little Engine That Could* by Watty Piper, expresses the mind-set that schools need to instill in students. To enhance a student's self-concept is to enhance his or her learning capacities.

This book was developed to provide teachers with activities, techniques and strategies for the enhancement of self-concept. We have included activities and ideas, which the teacher can use in the classroom within any framework. It is important to remember, however, that teachers' attitudes and the classroom atmosphere they create play a very large part in whether or not the activities prove useful and successful. The children will pick up a teacher's enthusiasm. If these activities are used in a positive and warm environment, the children have a better chance of developing into individuals who are glad to be themselves.

COMMUNICATING WITH YOURSELF

Teachers have been advised for many years to be warm, positive, supportive, patient, and caring individuals. A major difficulty is created when the classroom teacher attempts to put these vague suggestions into specific actions. It is necessary for each individual to understand these terms and to be able to implement this understanding in a consistent manner.

Any approach to education that does not consider individual differences of teachers is lacking an important dimension. Factors such as experiential background, teaching community, personality, culture, education, and values affect the way teachers use time, materials, and space. In addition, the above elements greatly influence personal teaching style.

Consider your own background, personality, culture, education, and values to determine *your* definitions of such specific terms as discipline, classroom management, rewards, punishments, and any other problems that require understanding and action.

Example: What does discipline mean to you? Sentences that begin with "If you know what's good for you . . ." "If you don't stop that immediately I'll. . ." "Who do you think you are?" "Do I have to call your mother?"

These are examples of the power struggle that can go on between teacher and child. When the power play begins, the battle is usually lost. The teacher loses in possibly two ways. In the first instance, the child does not back down and the teacher loses. Or, the child appears to submit to authority and actually seeks subtle ways to subvert the teacher's intentions.

Sentences that begin with:

"I like the way Susan is sitting . . ." "When you think you are ready you may rejoin the group." (Time out) "Show me how you can . . ." "I see you're having a problem there, why don't you come over and try this." (Redirection)

Each of these statements is non-threatening and provides options the child can exercise. Although there are situations when authority is necessary (health and safety), the ultimate goal of discipline is to help a child become independent and self-directing. Posing questions to children that require them to take responsibility for their actions will usually enhance feelings of self-worth. In Chapters Two and Three you will find other suggestions for using positive approaches.

How do you feel about you? If you feel good about yourself, you are on your way to helping children feel good about themselves. *Your* self-image is of primary importance.

A teacher who feels comfortable with creative activities will usually reflect this feeling in his or her daily routine. As a result, the children will have many opportunities to experience the creative arts.

Conversely, a teacher who does not feel competent in math or science will probably "avoid it like the plague." The children will receive both verbal and nonverbal messages that these subjects are difficult and boring and therefore should be avoided. If you find yourself in this situation where you consistently ignore a particular area in your curriculum, there are steps you can take to remedy this problem.

1. Use a discovery approach.
2. Use manipulative materials.
3. Be a facilitator rather than a lecturer.
4. Use open-ended questions that encourage children to think for themselves.
5. Over-plan so that you always have more than enough to do.
6. Don't be afraid to be wrong.
7. Talk to a teacher in your building who enjoys the areas you don't.
8. Take the lead from your children and follow their interests.

IMPLICATIONS
FOR THE CLASSROOM TEACHER

Developing positive self-images has many implications for the classroom teacher, and there are several techniques that can be used in an ongoing manner. A primary purpose for enhancing self-concept is to develop a sense of responsibility and independence in the child. The child who is resourceful and can cope with a variety of problems usually has had experiences that lead him to believe he is a worthwhile person and that he has some degree of control over his own life.

Teachers should encourage children to make decisions and to act on their decisions. Children should also be encouraged to do for themselves those tasks of which they are capable. Selection of the initial tasks should be made with an understanding of the child's interests and abilities.

To help children become responsible, begin with simple tasks and work up to more difficult ones as their skills increase. Some examples of preschool and kindergarten tasks for young children are listed below.

Self

Button, zip, tie, put on clothing
Hang up coats, hats
Encourage children to help others
Find things that get misplaced
Take care of personal needs
Send *verbal* messages with children for materials to be brought to class. Expect the child to relay the message, but be ready to provide for those who don't!

Classroom Care

Clean up:
washing tables, easels, paint brushes
Polishing, dusting, vacuuming, sweeping, mopping
Organizing, straightening storage areas
Room responsibilities:
wash tables, water plants, turn off lights

Daily Routine

Children need to discover, explore, experience cooking
cut, spread, with plastic or table knives
wash/dry pots, pans, dishes, silverware
open cans, bottles, packages
use appliances safely (toaster, can opener, mixer)
stir, mix

Use a camera, record player, tape recorder, filmstrip projector

Snacktime:
   pass out snack, napkins, cups—serve, pour
   clean up spills

Art:
   take out/put away own materials: scissors, glue, paper
   hang up easel paintings
   put name or symbol on project
   collect papers

Children plan:
   activities, projects, parties
   field trips, unit topics, choose songs, books
   make decisions, choices

Classroom Organization:
   Plan room set-up—where does our equipment go/fit best?
   Put together new equipment
   Create bulletin boards—children should have a part in every board—bulletin boards are *for* the children

Recall or Daily Evaluation:
   One child each day is in charge of asking his friends "What did you do today? Did you have a good day?"

Circle Time/Reading Group:
   Children can take turns being teacher and conducting circle activities:
      choosing jobs, child of the day, fingerplays, etc.

When establishing the environment and integrating those techniques into your curriculum, you will be helped by recalling a simple thought—"Never tell a child something he can discover for himself." (Joseph Pestalozzi)

2
Creating a Positive
Learning Environment

The classroom atmosphere you create as a teacher for young children has a great impact on the development of their self-concepts. When you establish an environment that encourages warmth, love, and cooperation, you will enhance the feelings your students have about themselves.

Evaluate your classroom atmosphere. Is there room for improvement? You might like to try some of the following suggestions for building positive feelings of self-worth within your own classroom. Once you begin, we hope that you'll soon be adding your own ideas to this guide.

1. Do you provide opportunities, early in the school year, for children to get to know each other? ____yes ____no
2. Do you make an effort to learn students' names as quickly as possible? ____yes ____no
3. When you speak to young children, do you physically come down to their level? ____yes ____no
4. Do you establish rapport by nonverbal as well as verbal communication? ____yes ____no
5. Do you help children understand your routine and your expectations of them so that they feel secure? ____yes ____no
6. Do you instill in each child a sense of belonging to the group? ____yes ____no
7. Do you accept each child's differences—his values, background, culture? ____yes ____no
8. Do you treat each child as an individual? Children of the same age differ greatly. ____yes ____no
9. Do you help students develop an awareness of individual differences and the acceptance of those differences? ____yes ____no
10. Do you help children to realize their individuality? ____yes ____no
11. Do you focus on the positive aspects of each child? ____yes ____no
12. Do you believe there is good in every child? ____yes ____no
13. Do you communicate a genuine interest in each child? ____yes ____no
14. Do you create an atmosphere of warmth and love by being kind, cheerful, and even-tempered? ____yes ____no

15. Have you found that children are more apt to listen carefully to a whisper than to a yell? ____yes ____no

16. Do you give children opportunities to display their talents? ____yes ____no

17. Do you display all papers and art work, not just the best? ____yes ____no

18. Do you give children opportunities to work and play in large and small groups as well as independently? ____yes ____no

19. Do you plan for children to learn from each other? ____yes ____no

20. Do the children in your classroom make plans and choices? ____yes ____no

21. Do you encourage children to share their ideas and to respect the differing ideas of others? ____yes ____no

22. Do you allow children to freely express themselves? ____yes ____no

23. Do you encourage children to solve their own problems? ____yes ____no

24. Do you interpret and label the feelings of children? Feelings are meant to be expressed, both positive and negative. Do you encourage this expression? ____yes ____no

25. Are you flexible and able to flow with the children's interests even when they don't coincide with your lesson plan? ____yes ____no

26. Do you build lessons on the experiences of your children? ____yes ____no

27. Do you reward and encourage attempts at achievement? ____yes ____no

28. Do you express positive encouragement of independence as well as helping after having assisted several times? ____yes ____no

29. Do you help children with difficult tasks? ____yes ____no

30. Do you know when to stand back and let children try their own wings? ____yes ____no

31. Do you help students identify and gain insight into their own problems and anxieties? ____yes ____no

32. Are you a friend to your students? ____yes ____no

33. Do you help children to discover and to understand their wants, needs, fears, and dreams? Are you accepting of all of these? ____yes ____no

34. Do you provide time for socialization and encourage friendship? ___yes ___no
35. Do you help children develop body awareness? ___yes ___no
36. Do you provide opportunities for children to learn about themselves and others? ___yes ___no
37. Do you set consistent, realistic, and challenging goals for children and teach them to do the same for themselves? ___yes ___no
38. Do you greet the children each day and comment on haircuts, new clothes, etc.? ___yes ___no
39. Do you make an effort to be aware of the special events in the lives of the children: birthdays, new babies? ___yes ___no
40. Are you a good model for children to follow? ___yes ___no
41. Are you a good listener? ___yes ___no
42. When there really isn't enough time to listen to a child, do you make sure that you get back to him sometime that same day? ___yes ___no
43. Do your students feel they are respected and liked, simply because they exist? ___yes ___no
44. Do you encourage children to show affection? ___yes ___no
45. Do you foster creativity? ___yes ___no
46. Do you encourage children to help each other? ___yes ___no
47. Do you establish a level of trust among class members? Do children trust you? ___yes ___no
48. Are you honest with children so that they learn honesty? ___yes ___no
49. Can you laugh at yourself in front of the children? ___yes ___no
50. Can you accept each child at his own emotional, social, physical, and intellectual level and build his education from those levels? ___yes ___no
51. Are you "up" on the stages of development of young children so that you can teach for success instead of failure? ___yes ___no
52. Do you encourage children to be aware and sensitive to their own "special-ness" and that of others? ___yes ___no
53. Do you notice children who would rather be helpers than doers? ___yes ___no
54. Do you give genuine and realistic praise? ___yes ___no

55. Do you encourage children to praise themselves when help is offered to provide a model? ___yes ___no
56. Do you realistically praise a helpful child and comment when a child praises himself? ___yes ___no
57. Do you withhold judgments and attempt to understand first, your student's reactions, responses and behavior? ___yes ___no
58. Do you try to be fair, consistent, and impartial when disciplining? ___yes ___no
59. Do you strive to help children evaluate their own behavior and the consequences of their actions? ___yes ___no
60. Do you make an effort to know family situations? ___yes ___no
61. Do you make parents partners in the education of their children? ___yes ___no
62. Do you provide a link between home and school with newsletters, phone calls, home visits, parent meetings, and/or conferences? ___yes ___no
63. Are you willing to educate the parents of your students to their role in developing the positive self-image in their children? ___yes ___no
64. Are parents welcome in your classroom? ___yes ___no
65. Are you now aware of your significant role in the development of the child's self-concept? ___yes ___no

SUMMARY

If you are reading this, you must feel good enough about yourself to say, "I can improve. My classroom atmosphere and management techniques could be better." Anyone who denies that fools himself. We can all be stimulated by new ideas. So you want a change? Then it's time you got started!

All the activities mentioned in this book will not help you to enhance young self-concepts if they are not presented in a positive, warm and loving atmosphere. This kind of learning environment must exist every day. The way you interact daily with young children has the greatest impact on the development of the self-concept. Positive self-images do not just happen. They must be nurtured along and tended carefully each day for growth to take place.

Some questions from the guide have easy solutions. If you're not doing what is suggested, give it a try. Other suggestions will easily fit into the teaching and management techniques you already use. Some improvements are harder to make and the book's activities should help you.

There are some tougher questions you know you'd like to solve, but just don't know how to go about doing the right thing. For instance, how do we help children get to know each other and what for? We provide projects, activities, group work, and social experiences that enable children to interact with each other. As a result they often make friends. Friendship promotes good feelings about self. See, you already know many of the answers!

When we mention good things about children and give recognition to a child, we instill in that child a sense of belonging. Be sure each student knows that *you* know he's there every day. Write yourself notes that remind you of things to compliment children on. If you find your day zipping by so quickly that there just isn't time, put the following sign above your classroom door.

Teacher, did you touch each child today?
With your eyes? With your voice?
With your hands? With your heart?

If not, do it now. For once they
pass through this door, you may never
have the chance again.

Terry Lynne Graham

Are there days when you *know* that your classroom atmosphere is not warm and loving and the reason is that *you* don't feel very warm and loving? We all have those days, it's normal. Try putting yourself in the children's place. If you were a child, would you want *you* for a teacher? If not, then brighten up! Relax! Everything eventually gets done and nothing is worth getting so uptight about that you hurt your children as well as yourself. Their days with you are so short. What kind of an impression will you leave with them?

"Help! I can't let kids freely express themselves. They go crazy, get out of control." You can do it. Expressing freely doesn't mean without rules, limitations, respect for others, and just plain good manners. Give your children rules and be consistent in your disciplinary measures. Children want discipline.

Free expression does mean accepting the way children think and feel. It means accepting what they say and how they say it. Sometimes children's language needs to be reworded or restated. They need you to label their feelings and to let them know that you share those same feelings sometimes too. Give children the opportunity for expression and remember that it doesn't have to be verbal. Art, music, poetry, and dance provide avenues for free expression.

When problems and conflicts do arise, asking, "What do you think we should do about that?" gives children a chance to find solutions to their own problems. But it is just as important to keep quiet and let things work themselves out. You are just as valuable as an observer as you are a mediator.

Never understimate the ability of your students to work things out. Even the very young have a feel for solving problems. Many questions from the guide could be discussed with your students. Ask them how you can be a better listener, or a better friend to them. Listen and record their recommendations. Children can be your teachers, too!

When we treat and teach children as individuals, we encourage individuality. When we show affection, we are telling children who are having genuine difficulties, we are teaching them to help themselves and to patiently help others. Teachers are models. Teachers are the steppingstones upon which children will build their self-concepts. How will the children in your class remember the year they spent with you?

3

Classroom Organization and Management

Before you can begin to organize your classroom, you must know your children. It is important that you are aware of their needs, interests, and experiences. A knowledge of child growth and development is essential.

Children thrive in a working situation when they are given opportunities to help plan and evaluate some of their activities. In this book, the activities we stress will help to enhance the self-concept of children. The ideas presented for record keeping and evaluation can be used in many subject areas.

When organizing your classroom it is important to remember that children learn in many ways. They should be given ample opportunity to work with a variety of materials and in different types of situations. Children should be given the opportunity to work as part of the total group, in small groups, and as individuals. The furniture in your room should be arranged for the three types of activities. In classrooms where desks are used, the desks may be placed in the center of the room or to one side. With this arrangement the centers may be placed around the perimeter of the room.

Blackboard

Bulletin Board
Art Corner

Individual Work Area

Library

Bulletin Board
Reading Center

Bulletin Board
Listening Center

Teacher's Desk

Desk

Piano

Music Area

Science Center

Math Center

Construction Area

Children need experiences in working in the total group situation so they can learn to listen to each other and to interact with others. Through the total group situation they also learn to share experiences and to build a foundation for future interaction. Children are also able to develop self-confidence by frequent opportunities to express themselves in the total group situation.

Small group interaction is also essential to the growth of young children. Small group work enables the children to feel they are active participants in the learning process. They are given more opportunities for leadership and follower roles when participating in this type of activity.

At times children need to be alone and work independently. While working independently, the children are able to work at their own pace and level. They are also able to develop a feeling of self-worth and confidence in their own abilities.

A sense of orderliness is essential when organizing your classroom. The furniture should be arranged to make the utmost use of space and to allow for free movement of the children. You should allow for movement from one center or area to another without having children interrupt each other.

Active centers should not be placed next to centers requiring relative quiet for concentration and understanding. When setting up centers it is essential to have bulletin boards or pinning space nearby so it can be utilized for center materials.

Teachers should also provide for the care and maintenance of materials. There should be a place for each item to be stored and the children should be aware of this.

TEACHER PLANNING—
PRE-SCHOOL AND KINDERGARTEN

We all need a plan. Some of us need to write things in detail, and others jot notes here and there on scraps of paper. Planning is time-consuming, but very necessary. The following plans give children a daily routine so that they will feel confident and know what to expect. *Teacher's Planning Record #1* lists activities that the children will experience daily. For example, small group time

Teacher's Preschool Planning Record #1 — Daily Routine

Date _____

CIRCLE TIME	SMALL GROUP TIME	CHILD PLANNING	RECALL TIME
9:30/1:00	10:00/1:30	10:45/1:45	11:10/2:40

Greeting Song
Attendance, Jobs
Special Child, Calendar
Weather
	KEY EXPERIENCE
	
	Materials
		Work Time
		    10:30-11:00
		    2:00-2:30
			Method

Rhymes		Clean Up	SELF-CONCEPT ACTIVITY
Fingerplays		Snack	
Concepts		11:20/2:50 Prepare to go home 11:55/3:25 Goodbye Song Notes Hugs, etc.	

LANGUAGE ARTS Includes stories, filmstrips, poetry	GROSS MOTOR/MOVEMENT/MUSIC/ BODY AWARENESS	SPECIAL ACTIVITIES — NOTES

OBSERVATIONS

EVALUATIONS

Teacher's Planning Record #2 —
Daily Routine

Date _____

ROUTINE	OBJECTIVE	MATERIALS/ACTIVITIES	OBSERVATIONS	EVALUATION
CIRCLE TIME 9:00/1:00	KEY EXPERIENCE			
SMALL GROUP 10:00/1:30				
CHILD PLAN 10:15/1:45				
WORK TIME 10:20/1:50				
CLEAN UP 11:00/2:30				
RECALL 11:10/2:40				
SNACK — 11:15/2:45				
GROSS MOTOR OUTSIDE 11:30/3:00				
SPECIAL ACTIVITIES				
COMMENTS				

provides students with closer attention from adults. Self-image activities are perfect for small group time. During work time (you may call it play time, free time) larger groups can use centers and areas that deal with enhancing self-concept. An art activity, such as self-portraits, can be presented to the group and then put in the art area. The children may choose that activity, or they may go to other activities. Allowing the choice is important.

Circle time provides an opportunity to share the poems, finger-plays, and stories that foster self-image growth. Remember to close the day with daily evaluations. Questions help children bring their day together and let them go home with a feeling of time enjoyed and well spent.

CHILD PLANNING

Preschool and kindergarten children are capable of planning their daily activities. When you have introduced all the areas or centers of the room and they have had some experiences with materials, the children are ready to make their daily plans.

"What would you like to do today, John?" opens the plan period. John may point to an area or he may say, "I'd like to go to the Block Area." Accept the manner in which a child plans and build upon it. Gradually ask for more detail. "What do you think you'll build, John, and what materials will you need?"

There are various ways to make plans depending upon the abilities of your students. Some children will draw daily plans, others will dictate plans to you, and some may only point or gesture.

The *Preschool or Kindergarten Planning Record #1* shows how every child plans and the areas he works in. The numbers under the areas tell John's plan in sequence. John is encouraged to follow his plan in sequence. Plans are carried out during Work Time.

The last category, Recall Time, is a time for getting the children together to find out what they can tell you about their daily experiences. Whether they remember their activities in order, what details they can express, and the areas frequented tell you a lot about each child. This record provides you with an account of each child's daily progress. The recall of activities can also be represented in art or drama.

Preschool Planning Record #1

Name _JOHN_

DATE	AREAS/ACTIVITIES									
	House	Blocks	Sand/ Water	Art/ Easel	Quiet	Cooking	Music	Climb	Constr.	Recall
3-7-81	2	1	3							
—										
—										
—										
—										
—										
—										
—										
—										
—										
—										
—										
—										
—										
—										
—										
—										
—										
—										
—										
—										
—										
—										

Child Planning Record #2 is another method of record keeping. Many room materials and the areas are listed here. Teachers and adults working in the classroom observe the child as he completes his plan and check areas and materials the child uses.

25

Child Planning Record #2

DAY	MONDAY	TUESDAY	WEDNESDAY	THURSDAY	FRIDAY
PLAN					
Blocks					
Trucks					
Serv. Sta.					
Trains					
Phones					
Kitchen					
Dress-up					
Dolls					
Books					
Puzzles					
Pegs					
Lego Blocks					
Bristle Bl.					
Misc.					
Playdough					
Hamsters					
Scissors					
Water/Paint					
Crayons					
Easel					
Sand/Water					
Workbench					
Misc.					
Clean-up					
Recall					
Circle I					
Small group					
Circle II					
Activity time					
COMMENTS					

RECORD KEEPING

The *Child Observation Record* that follows is a device that aids the teacher in charting a child's daily progress in the areas of language, behavior and attitude, and achievement. Teachers can add other curriculum areas to the sheet. A card file with a four-by-six card for each student can also be an effective record-keeping technique. As often as possible, jot notes on the cards. Note good days and bad, successes, and skills that you have observed a child may need help to master.

Child Observation Record

Date	Language	Behavior or Attitude	Achieve-ments	Additional Comments	Recommen-dations
Monday					
Tuesday					
Wednesday					
Thursday					
Friday					

TEACHER PLANNING—
GRADES ONE THROUGH FOUR

Primary grade teachers usually do their planning when completing their daily or weekly planbooks. The following individual and group checklists are additional ways to help the teacher in planning for the use of the various centers in the room. They also afford an opportunity for individual planning with the children. The checklists may be expanded or amended to suit the needs of the children and the teacher.

Children will begin using the checklists as soon as they display sufficient independence and the necessary skills. The checklist may be kept by the teacher, displayed in interest centers, or kept in the children's individual folders.

The most important thing to remember is that the children must know what is expected of them and they must understand the direction and use of the materials for each learning center activity. Activities may be presented and explained to the whole group or to small groups. The activities and materials may then be placed in the centers for later use by the children. Some of the activities may also be worked on by the whole group at one time depending on the format of your classroom.

Center Checklist (Daily) #1

CHILD'S NAME   CENTERS USED

	Math	Listening Center	Art	Reading	Science
John	✓		✓		
Sue		✓			
Anthony			✓	✓	
Peggy	✓				✓
Michael	✓	✓			✓
Jane			✓		

Individual Center Checklist (Weekly) #2

	SCIENCE	MATH	READING	ART	LISTENING CENTER
Monday					
Tuesday					
Wednesday					
Thursday					
Friday					

EVALUATION

Evaluation in the primary grades may take many forms. It can be a simple checklist, a conference between teacher and child, teacher observation, or written or oral comments by the child. A conference between teacher and child should include several questions.

> What has the child learned?
> Why did the child choose this activity?
> Did the child enjoy the activity?
> What did the activity make the child aware of?

Teachers may expand on the questions asked to suit the needs of the child and the activity completed.

Teacher observation should include the following questions. Again the suggested ideas may be expanded or things omitted as needed.

> What centers is the child using?
> Are the activities appropriate for the child?
> Is the child's performance in the area improving?
> Is the child utilizing more than one or two centers in a week?

A self-evaluation may also be completed by the child. After completing an activity, each child may express how he felt about it, what he learned about himself or others, and what was learned

Center Work

Name _____

Date _____

I plan to do this today	COMPLETED	NOT COMPLETE
MATH CENTER	✓	
SCIENCE CENTER		✓

Teacher Checklist

MATH CENTER — Please correct mistakes circled.

or

Math Center Work	
	Correct this please
	Complete this please
✓	Please see me!!!

from the experience. These expressions may be oral, written, or taped for later examination by the teacher.

Children who are able to express themselves through writing may keep a small notebook or personal journal evaluating their activities. Each child records his reactions and expresses his feelings about the activity. The journal becomes an ongoing record of the child's progress and growth.

Another means of evaluation can be the *Thought/Feelings* chart illustrated. The chart may be duplicated or kept in a journal. The child should be given time to fill in the chart upon completing each activity.

Evaluation #1—Thought/Feelings Chart

DATE	ACTIVITY	I THINK . . .	I FEEL . . .

Children may devise their own chart or you may ditto a chart. Children should update the chart after each activity.

Open-ended sentences may also be used for evaluation. Young children may use pictures or circle alternative answers to complete the sentences as shown in the second evaluation form, while older children may complete the sentences on their own.

Evaluation #2

ACTIVITY

1. It was fun for me because I _____
   felt happy   felt sad   learned much

2. I enjoyed completing the activity because _____
   it was fun   I learned a lot   It made me think

3. I was bored because I _____
   felt sad   I didn't learn much   didn't like the activity

4. Next time I will _____
   try harder   choose something different

Happy   Sad

Learned
a lot

Didn't learn
much

Bored

SUMMARY

Many suggestions have been made concerning classroom management and organization, but only you as the teacher can put them to work. It is important to create an atmosphere that is cheerful, warm, and comfortable so that both you and the children are able to enjoy working and interacting. As the teacher, you are the most important aspect of good organization and management in the classroom. Only you can create a wholesome atmosphere where children can grow, discover new things and develop a positive self-image.

As the teacher, you should be prepared. Have clear, specific purposes for your lessons and centers, but be flexible. There are times when all the planning should be forgotten—the needs of the children come first. Try to motivate and maintain interest in the learning situation. Use variety in presenting your activities. Use your voice wisely, remembering that children readily react to your voice. Make sure of the children's progress. Establish goals for your lessons and activities.

Remember *you* set the tone of your classroom. *You* can make it work.

4

Parents and Children Working and Learning Together

"Can I help you Daddy, Mommy?,"
Our little ones may say.
"No, run along," we answer, "you'll just be in the way."
They only want to share our time, to be with us a while,
To work, to play, to learn our ways,
To laugh, to touch, to smile.
If we spend time together, throughout their growing years,
And answer all their questions, and comfort all their tears,
They may remember what we shared
Was more valuable than gold,
A lot of love, a little time, a precious memory to hold.

Terry Lynne Graham

The monthly *Together* activities in this chapter are divided into Preschool/Kindergarten and Elementary sections and are designed to help parents enhance the child's self-image in the home. Because parents are the child's first and most influential teachers, the atmosphere they create for the child has the greatest impact on the child's feelings of self-worth.

These activities allow parents and children to "get in touch" with each other through art, poetry, cooking, nature experiences, language, and literature. A *Message From Your Child* at the end of each monthly letter, helps parents tune into the feelings, abilities, and development of their young children.

September—Together

Dear Parents,

September brings new beginnings for you and your child. We can all work together to make the first school experience a positive one. Here are some activities you both can do at home to help your child get off on the right foot, feel good about himself or herself, and carry on learning at home.

1. Trace your child's footprint here. Keep it and compare it with growth in June. Record his or her height and weight.

FOOTPRINTS

Date _____

_____ Weight _____
_____ Height _____

2. Set aside a "talking time" each day to discuss school happenings. Be sure to ask specific questions: Where did you play today? Who worked with you? And most important, "Did you have a good day?"

*Enlarge letter on a piece of paper 8½ x 11 so footprint can be drawn in.

Reading Together

Who Are You? by Joan Behrens
Why Me? by Nancy Mack
First Day in School by Bill Binzen

A Message From Your Child:

> *Praise my efforts*
> *I can do some things easily and well*
> *Some things are still hard for me*
> *I do not have to be good at everything now*
> *I can make some mistakes*
> *Praise my efforts, please*

Enjoy your child's growing years.

Sincerely,

Your Child's Teacher

COMMENTS

October—Together

Dear Parents,

Fall is a good time to take note of the many beautiful changes taking place in nature and to share them with your child. Children are changing, too. Our children are becoming more independent and responsible. They are observing their environments, making friends, making planning choices, and making choices. Encourage your child to share these changing times with you.

1. Take a nature walk together. Collect leaves, bits of bark, and stones. Talk about how each item feels, looks, and smells. Look for animals and listen for sounds. Pose questions. Answer questions.
2. Children feel proud of themselves when they accomplish new skills. Give them responsibilities at home and a chance to progress and succeed. Use stars, stickers, or checks.

Jobs _____

	Mon.	Tues.	Wed.	Thurs.	Fri.	Sat.	Sun.
Making my bed							
Brushing teeth							
Going to bed on time							
Putting toys away							
Getting along							
Other							

Reading Together

The Yucky Monster by Arthur Roth
Sometimes I'm Afraid by Jane Werner Watson
Will I Have a Friend? by Miriam Cohen

A Message From Your Child:

> *Talk with me. No one can know what I think or how I feel unless I tell them*
> *My thoughts and ideas are important*
> *Give me an awareness of nature*

SPECIAL NOTE

Halloween is a special time for children. It can be fun, but for young children it can also be a frightening time. Help your child to understand his or her fears. They are normal and need to be discussed and accepted. Fears are not silly. They are real. Be very patient.

Sincerely,

Your Child's Teacher

Dear Parents,

Our home activities this month focus on Thanksgiving and the family. Here are some ideas for helping your child feel a part of the Thanksgiving festivities.

1. Consult your child when planning your special feast. What would he or she like to see on the menu? Do your shopping together. Prepare a shopping list. Let your child illustrate it. It takes more time but it's worth it!

2. Trace around your child's hand to create a turkey. He or she can add legs, eyes, and color the feathers. Be sure to give that turkey a name!

3. Placemats: Enhance your table with homemade placemats. Cut pictures from magazines that express things for which we are thankful. Place them between two sheets of wax paper and press with a warm iron. You can use clear contact paper instead if you want the placemats to last. Add family snapshots too!

Reading Together

I Can Do It by Muriel Stanek
My Family by Miriam
Little Bear's Thanksgiving by Mariane

A Message From Your Child:

I am loveable
I can learn to love others
I have the right to my childhood
I learn to think, feel and express myself by watching you

For this child, we are truly thankful.

Sincerely,

Your Child's Teacher

Dear Parents,

There are many exciting things to do together at this time of year. It's also a good time to talk about the needs and feelings of others, giving, and sharing.

1. Encourage your child to make his or her own gifts. Children's own art work is a meaningful gift that they can share with others. Your child's photographs in an album he or she has created, make a wonderful gift. Ask your child to dictate to you his or her thoughts about each photo.

2. Show your child how to wrap his or her own gifts. Children take pride in their accomplishments, and cutting, taping, and tying are great for fine muscle coordination.

3. Save your holiday cards for cutting and pasting. Just ask, "What do you think we could do with this?"

Reading Together

Love is a Special Way of Feeling by Joan Walsh Anglund
I Have Feelings by Terry Berger
How Santa Claus Had a Long and Difficult Journey Delivering His Presents (a textless delight) by Fernando Krahn
Look out the Window by Joan Walsh Anglund

A Message From Your Child:

I'm me. I'm special. No one is just like me.
I am like others in some ways, but I am still very different.
Please don't compare me with my brothers, sisters, or friends.
Others need to know I'm special. Talk me up!
Help me to know that others are special in their own way too.

HAPPY HOLIDAYS!

Sincerely,

Your Child's Teacher

Dear Parents,

You'll be spending long hours indoors during the winter months. Try some cooking activities to spice up those chilly days. Remember that your child can do much of the stirring, mixing, measuring, and of course, cleaning up!

PLAYDOUGH

Mix and knead: 1 cup salt
1½ cups flour
2 Tbl. cooking oil

Use more flour to avoid stickiness. Add food coloring. Store in refrigerator in plastic bag or jar. Add more oil to make pliable again.

GINGERBREAD PEOPLE

1 cup butter	5 cups sifted flour
1 cup sugar	1½ tsp. salt
1 egg	2 tsp. ginger
1 cup molasses (dark)	1 tsp. cinnamon
2 Tbl. vinegar	1 tsp. cloves

Cream butter, add sugar gradually. Blend in egg, molasses, and vinegar. Blend in dry ingredients. Chill. Roll out ⅛ to ¼ inch thick on lightly greased sheet. Cut into shapes with cookie cutters. Use raisins and cinnamon candies for face or buttons. Bake at 375° for 5 to 15 minutes depending on thickness.

Be sure to talk about textures, fragrances, flavors, colors and shapes.

Reading Together

The Gingerbreadman by Ed Arno
Mike's House by Julia Saver
Too Many Mittens by Louis Slobodkin
The Snowy Day by Ezra Jack Keats

A Message From Your Child:

*Remember that I can do many things that I couldn't do when I
    was a baby*
Help me to accept the things that I am not yet ready to do
I learn by doing, exploring, and discovering
I can learn to do things by myself
Be patient with me

Take a winter walk. Discuss the changes you see.

Sincerely,

Your Child's Teacher

February—Together

Dear Parents,

February is a special month for expressing our warm feelings for
each other. Help your child to know how you feel about him or her
and show your child ways to express his or her feelings for you.

1. Make valentines. Cut hearts from magazines, news, and
wrapping paper. Tell your child the things he or she does that
make you happy—the little things. Let your child know that
even when you are angry with him or her that you still love him
or her.

2. Heart-shaped sandwiches:
Freeze several slices of bread. Use cookie cutters to form
shapes from the bread. Whip 8 oz. cream cheese with
2 Tbl. of milk. Add red food coloring. Spread on bread.

3. Look for magazine pictures of families showing their love
for one another in different ways.

Reading Together

A Friend is Someone Who Likes You by Joan Walsh Anglund
Around and Around Love by Betty Miles
Do You Love Someone? by Joan Walsh Anglund

A Message From Your Child:

> *Listen to me*
> *My thoughts are important*
> *When I share my own ideas or do things in my own way,*
> *I am being creative*
> *I know that I make you angry sometimes,*
> *but weren't you a kid once?*

Sincerely,

Your Child's Teacher

March—Together

Dear Parents,

Children learn so much from television, both positive and negative. Parents and teachers need to help them choose appropriate programs and limit TV time. Skim the TV guide each week for special children's programs. Then, watch them together!

1. Discuss programs.
   Which characters do you like? Why? Who didn't you like?
   Who would you like to be?
   How did the program begin? End?
   Were there sad, happy, and funny parts?
   Tell me the story again. Tell me the story from the point of view of one of the characters.

2. Many children know the game show routine very well. Dramatize it together. A cardboard paper roll can serve as a microphone for the M.C. It's a game that can easily be played

when you're busy doing other things. Make up questions for each other. "Family Feud" and "Hollywood Squares" are favorites. And don't forget to mention the prizes that can be won!

Be sure to take time from TV for:

Reading Together

Spring is the Nicest Time of Year by Gay Zhenya
The Book of Me by Dean Walley
Who's That in the Mirror? by Polly Berends

A Message From Your Child:

Give me your attention before I'm all grown up
Give me your respect so that I can learn to respect myself
Give me the opportunity to develop a sense of humor
<u>*Give me your love so that I may give it back to you*</u>

Sincerely,

Your Child's Teacher

April—Together

Dear Parents,

Your child has been growing socially, intellectually, and emotionally, with your help and guidance. I hope your time spent together on the monthly activities has enhanced that growth and given you an understanding of your child's development. Our experiences for you this month deal with body awareness and feelings.

1. Me Doll:
   Child adds facial features and colors clothes. Pinking shears can be used to cut the doll into puzzle parts.

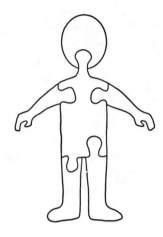

2. Have child close eyes. Take one piece of the puzzle away. What's missing?

3. Cover doll with clear Contact paper to preserve it.

Reading Together

Spring is a New Beginning by Joan Walsh Anglund
Miss Suzy's Easter Surprise by Arnold Loebel
I Was So Mad by Norma Simon

A Message From Your Child:

People like me when I'm friendly.
Even when I'm not friendly, I am still myself. I'm being me.
Sometimes I'm not proud of what I have done. I feel happier if I am allowed to help make things better by fixing what I have broken or cleaning up the messes I have made. Let me help you.

Sincerely,

Your Child's Teacher

Dear Parents,

While May flowers are springing up all around us, our children have also bloomed. We hope they are feeling good about themselves and feel that their feelings, both positive and negative, are acceptable. Our May activities explore feelings and encourage discussion concerning all feelings.

May Flowers:

Child's flowers—On each petal write something that makes you Happy, Sad, or Angry. Do the same for parent's flowers.

Reading Together

That Makes Me Mad by Steven Kroll
Leo the Late Bloomer by Robert Kraus
The Sesame Street Book of People and Things
Happy Sad Silly Mad by Barbara Hazen

A Message From Your Child:

> *Help me build on my strengths*
> *I do not like to do things that I cannot do well, do you?*
> *Sometimes I just need more time to grow and develop*
> *Sometimes I need special help*
> *I do want you to be proud of me. Did you know that?*
> *Allow me to be angry sometimes too.*
> <u>*I need to express my feelings like you do.*</u>

Sometimes it's hard to express your feelings to a child. They need to know that you are angry at times, just as they are.

Sincerely,

Your Child's Teacher

June—Together

Dear Parents,

As our school year closes, let's take a moment to look back at September. Think about the many ways your child has grown and progressed. Have you progressed, too?

I hope you have enjoyed working, playing, learning, and growing with your child. I have enjoyed you both. Thank you for taking the time and effort to be an active participant in your child's education.

1. Measure footprints

FOOTPRINTS

Date _____

2. Headlines:

   Help your child paste a small paper plate on construction paper. Ask him or her to draw a face and add a body. Cut words from the newspaper that describe him or her.

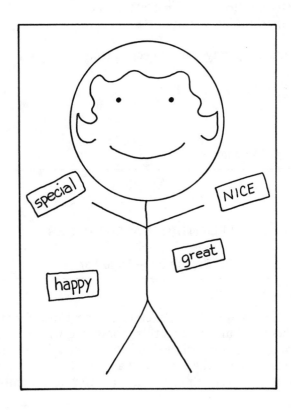

Reading Together

I'm Glad I'm Me by Elbeda Stone
I Know What I Like by Nova Simon
Alexander and the Terrible, Horrible, No Good,
    Very Bad Day by Judith Viorst

A Message From Your Child:

Love me
Let me grow and go
Encourage me. Guide me. Teach me.
Help me to know my limits. Don't give in to me.
Your discipline makes me know that you care
I know that you do not always have time for me
It is the quality of our time together that is
    important, not the quantity

You parents are pretty special people, too.

Sincerely,

Your Child's Teacher

ELEMENTARY PARENT PAGES

September—Together

Dear Parents,

Back-to-school means Back Together for our class. From the first day of school and all through this month, we will be working on projects and activities designed to help us get to know each other. While the children of the class have a great deal in common, each one is an individual with something to offer as a member of the group. We stress the importance of and the acceptance of individual differences within our class.

Ideas:

1. Explore with your child your family's history. Information about parents, grandparents, and other relatives can be both interesting and a source of pride to your child. A backward glance, even if brief, can give your child a sense of belonging and an idea of his or her place in the total family unit.

2. Record with your child his other accomplishments throughout the coming school year. These can be related to school work or on a personal level, such as learning to ride a bicycle or playing an instrument. Reaching a goal in home or family life should also be included. This record of tasks mastered can be used at the end of the school year to evaluate growth and progress as well as a source of pride in the jobs well done.

Books:

Just Only John by Jack Kent
The Book of Me by Dean Walley

Sincerely,

Your Child's Teacher

October—Together

Dear Parents,

The new season of autumn brings many changes and chances to observe the world around us. Our class will explore the obvious signs such as the colored leaves, the weather, the animals' behavior, and the changes in the amount of daylight. Changes and differences, although not so obvious, can be found within ourselves as well. Our class will be learning how people change and grow just as nature does. The topics we will cover include the physical as well as the emotional changes of attitudes and feelings.

Ideas:

1. Keep a height and weight chart for your child on a monthly basis. Stress the importance and relationship of good eating habits and the need for proper sleep and rest.

2. As Halloween approaches, plan with your child for this special celebration. It is an exciting and adventurous time, second only to Christmas. Working together to design a costume, making a plan of neighborhood visits, and deciding on what treats will be given out at your house will give your child a feeling of helpfulness and a sense of value. It stresses that he or she has something to offer and that he or she can be of help to others.

Books:

The Very Little Girls by Phyllis Kravilovsky
Hooray for Me by Lillian Moore

Sincerely,

Your Child's Teacher

November—Together

Dear Parents,

This is a busy month for school-related activities, with the first report card of the new school year, beginning of parent-teacher conferences, and the celebration of Thanksgiving. Our class will be working on projects and activities that explore the family background this month. During the month each child will be creating a "Me Book" that deals with his individual family and personal life. It is somewhat like a mini autobiography. Your help during this project will be appreciated.

Ideas:

1. Record with your child a family tree. Be sure to include grandparents, aunts, uncles, and cousins. As an extra touch you may try to include some interesting facts about the relatives such as place and year of birth, occupation, and even a picture.

2. Help your child gather material and information for his or her "Me Book." Children will need pictures (old and recent), lists of hobbies, sports, interests, and information regarding physical changes in height and weight.

Books:

Just Right by Lillian Moore
Who's That in the Mirror? by Polly Berends

Sincerely,

Your Child's Teacher

December—Together

Dear Parents,

This is a month filled with excitement, anticipation, wonder and delight, as well as a good opportunity to explore emotions and feelings with the children. Our class will be discovering, discussing, and learning about the many kinds of emotions. The goal of activities and projects for this month is to gain a better understanding and acceptance of feelings and emotions. It is hoped that this knowledge will aid in coping and dealing with the wide range of feelings that are evident within each child.

Ideas:

1. Create faces out of paper plates. Each plate could express a different emotion or feeling that your child has experienced. Discuss with your child when and why he or she felt that way as he or she draws and decorates the plate.

2. Begin a small notebook of feelings and emotions to record your child's reactions to new situations. Be prepared to talk over with your child emotions that may be confusing or even frightening to him or her. After several months, recall together the early entries and note how your child has changed and grown emotionally.

Books:

I Have Feelings by Terry Berger
The Boy with a Problem by Joan Fassler
Peter's Chair by Ezra Jack Keats
Sometimes I'm Afraid by Jane Watson Werner

Sincerely,

Your Child's Teacher

January—Together

Dear Parents,

A new year, a new month, and a new area of study for our class. During this long, cold month, the topic of discussion and activity will be the importance of being yourself. We will be exploring the things that make each of us an individual, with our own special attributes that make each of us a valuable member of the whole class. Setting some short-term goals, making some resolutions, and planning for the immediate future are three sections of study for this month.

Ideas:

1. Help your child select a goal that you and the rest of the family can help him or her accomplish. Be sure that it is something he or she is capable of and that will not take an

excessive amount of time. Some suggestions: learn how to ice skate, learn some magic tricks and put on a show, learn how to make a puppet, learn the times tables, etc. Remember, the whole idea is for the child to end up with a mastered task and a sense of pride and accomplishment.

2. Due to the winter weather, your family will be spending more time indoors during this month. Begin a collection of games, books, craft ideas, puzzles, and activities that your child is particularly fond of. Sharing these together helps to pass the long, cold winter and may come in handy on the rainy days of spring that are ahead.

Books:

   Miss Twiggley's Tree by Lillian Moore
   Just Me by Marie Hall Ets
   Fierce John by Edward Fenton

Sincerely,

Your Child's Teacher
_____

February—Together
_____

Dear Parents,

This is a short month that is highlighted by the anticipation and celebration of Valentine's Day. In addition to the traditional exchange of valentines and cards, our class will be exploring the various ways people have of showing and expressing their interest in and feelings for others. We will discuss the little ways that we can show and express our warm feelings for others, both in the school setting and at home. Taking time out to express our feelings and concerns for others leads to better understanding and rapport within the class as a whole.

Ideas:

1. Help your child design and create personal valentines to share with others. Aside from classmates, include relatives, neighbors, and other friends. Be sure to stress the acceptance of expressing personal feelings and the need to share these feelings with others.

2. Make a collage of magazine pictures or photographs that depict the various ways that people can express their warm feelings for others. Display the project in a prominent place for the entire family to share.

Books:

The Hating Book by Charlotte Zolotow
Sam by Ann Herbert Scott
Around and Around Love by Betty Miles

Sincerely,

Your Child's Teacher

March—Together

Dear Parents,

This month brings the end of the long, cold winter and the onset of spring. Our class will be observing and discussing the signs of spring, much in the same manner that we studied the beginning of autumn. Seen as a new beginning and a period of growth, spring lends itself to our class topics of personal growth and development. Building self-confidence and a feeling of competence are the goals of the projects and activities for this month. Stressing the strengths and working to improve the weaknesses of each individual builds a unity within the class as a whole.

Ideas:

1. Create a "Here's Spring" chart to compare the changes and signs of spring with your child's growth and development. Compare what the trees, flowers, and grass need to grow with the things necessary for your child to grow. Pictures of changes in plants and animals in spring can be compared to photographs that depict the changes in your child.

2. On St. Patrick's Day, discuss the ways in which your child considers himself or herself to be lucky or fortunate. Be sure to suggest family, friends, and his or her special abilities or skills.

Books:

Titch by Pat Hutchins
Big Enough by Sherry Kafka
Leo the Late Bloomer by Robert Kraus

Sincerely,

Your Child's Teacher

April—Together

Dear Parents,

During April our class, as well as our school, will be celebrating National Library Week. Perhaps the greatest academic change and growth to happen during each school year involves reading. During the early, formative years, reading and reading-related skills are stressed at each grade level. In our year-long attempt to nurture a positive self-concept, books have played an important role. The value of books is that they can provide both real and vicarious experiences from which the child can gain insight and understanding of himself or herself and of others.

Ideas:

1. Visit your local library with your child. They often provide a wide variety of programs free of charge. Get a library card for your child and offer ample opportunity for him or her to use it. Discover the wide variety of books available for young readers which, in addition to providing entertainment, help to enchance and foster a good self-image.

2. This month our class will participate in a "Bookmark Contest" to celebrate Library Week. Help your child create and design a personalized bookmark that expresses the joys of reading to your child.

Books:

The Important Book by Margaret Wise Brown
Fish is Fish by Leo Lionni
Look at Me Now by Robert E. Switzer
Horton Hears a Who! by Dr. Seuss

Sincerely,

Your Child's Teacher

May—Together

Dear Parents,

During our last whole month of school, our class will be trying to generate an interest in and an appreciation of the cultural differences that exist within our class. Having worked all year to expand and develop the individuality of each child, we have now reached the point of sharing. We will be exploring the culture, traditions, and foods of the various nationalities that are represented in our class. Fostering a better understanding of the different backgrounds can discourage prejudice and bias.

Ideas:

1. Help your child prepare a food dish that reflects his or her nationality. Prepare enough, if possible, to share with the class.

2. Find and read with your child books that are folktales or legends of his or her nationality. Books that explain culture or traditions are useful to enhance pride in your child's heritage.

Books:

In My Mother's House by Ann Nolan Clark
Your Skin and Mine by Paul Showers
Crow Boy by Taro Yashima

Sincerely,

Your Child's Teacher

June—Together

Dear Parents,

Another year draws to a close with a busy, active month. Now is a good time to reflect on the progress and effort put forth by both the children and the parents. Our objective during this year has been to explore, expand, and enhance each child's self-concept. The child gains insight and understanding of self and others through participation in physical-motor activities, social and emotional relationships, and cognitive experiences. A good self-concept can have an effect on academic achievement. During this summer, continue to have a sharing time together with your child.

Ideas:

1. Review and recall with your child the various charts and records kept during the school year. Be sure to stress the areas

of accomplishment and improvement. Continue to add new facts and information during the summer.

2. Help your child recreate his or her year in school in a month-by-month review. A booklet that recalls the memories, accomplishments, and crafts of each month could be made. Stress the gains and discoveries made each month.

Books:

A Silly Little Kid by Joe Feinstein
Look Out the Window by Joan Walsh Anglund
What Mary Jo Shared by Janice May Udry

Sincerely,

Your Child's Teacher

Fall

Summer

5

All Through the Year

Spring

Winter

Little seeds planted in the fall,
Need rain and sun, you know.

A child's self-image is a seed,
That needs nourishment to grow.

And so dear teacher, please remember,
The self-image you nurtured in September,

Needs your attention every day,
If you expect a flower to bloom in May.

Terry Lynne Graham

Fall is the time most of us devote to self-image development. We talk about family, body awareness, and the importance of personal-social relationships. Unfortunately, after the first few months of school, the development of *self* gets lost in the reading, math, and "get 'em ready for next year" shuffle. We are responsible for the total development of our students for a complete school year. Yet, we seldom nourish the one aspect of their development that has the greatest impact on their academic success: the self-image. We forget that being ready for next year, meeting the challenges of math and reading, all depend on the child's positive self-concept.

A child is very vulnerable. His self-concept is easily worn down because he does not understand why adults and peers in his life are not always kind, affectionate, reasonable, or fair. He believes he is at fault when he does not understand their motives and actions. When this happens, the child feels he is not right as a person. We must make sure our students feel right as people. We need to constantly rebuild and enhance feelings about self, not just in September, but year 'round.

Chapter Five provides experiences from September through June to help children feel good about themselves. The activities are group and independent studies, bulletin boards, and projects that can be worked on for the complete school year. These activities can be part of units and can be used anytime. "Helping Hands" and "I Am Special" should be part of your daily routine. Title a section of your plan book, "Self-Image Activity." Designate one bulletin board for "Self-Building." This will keep you aware of the importance of making self-image an integral part of your curriculum.

Don't forget to build self-image through your classroom atmosphere, too. You may use every activity in this book, but if the atmosphere your students work and learn in is not warm and supportive, the activities are meaningless.

The way you present and use our suggestions to develop positive self-images is up to you. Contrary to what we often hear, when helping children to have good feelings about themselves, we are concerned with the product, not with the process. We have supplied you with the ideas that we have found to be successful with young children. We hope you will add your own personal touches so that they best meet the needs of your students.

HELPING HANDS

The teacher sets up a center to list room responsibilities for the children. During the first week of school, trace each child's hand and cut them out. Older children will be able to do their own. Write names and for the not-yet-readers add a symbol they can recognize as their own. Make a chart listing responsibilities. When a child has a daily or weekly job, he uses a clothespin to secure his "Helping Hand" to the chart.

I AM SPECIAL—
CHILD OF THE DAY

Make each child special by taking turns as "Child of the Day."

You'll Need: ribbon, tag board, marker, hole punch

Here's How: Make a special necklace from the tag board. Write
I AM SPECIAL on it and punch a hole through it at the top. Thread
the ribbon through and tie. Have a box filled with students'
snapshots. Choose one each day to be the special child of the day.
Hang the picture in a special place and allow the child to wear the
necklace for that day. The chosen child may have special privileges
for the day. Other children dictate a chart of things that they like or
admire about the special child.

THE ME TREE

Start the year by having the children create a large tree that can
change with the seasons (sponge painting works well for fall or
spring). Use this tree as a "Me Tree" to display self-portraits.

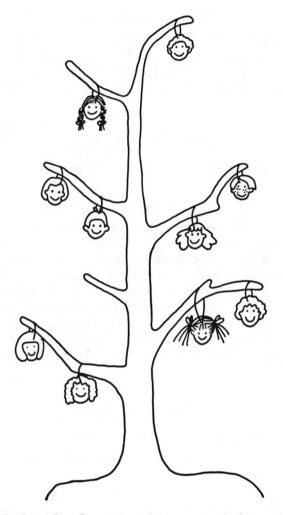

You'll Need: colored construction paper circles, crayons, hole punch, yarn, and paste

Here's How: Use the circle as a base for drawing a face. Use colored yarn for hair. Punch two holes at the top and thread yarn through. Hang on tree. With each change of season, children can recreate their pictures.

WELCOME, FRIEND

Develop specific ways to welcome new students into your class. Discuss how it might feel to be the "new kid." Discuss questions to ask of the new student, ways to help him feel more at ease, and maybe develop a sort of "buddy system" for new students.

SOMEBODY LIKES ME

A way for children to become more aware of personality traits in others.

You'll Need: large-size chart paper, crayons, drawing paper

Here's How: Ask the children to name a friend and to tell why they like that person. On chart paper, list the traits named. Read the list to the class and pause after each trait. Ask the children to stand if they feel that the trait describes them. Then identify the children who are standing as having that trait. A follow-up activity could be to have each child draw a friend. Have them also dictate or write what they like about that person. They should also tell why they think the other person likes them. Make booklets of responses and drawings entitled "Somebody Likes Me, Yes They Do."

THE "I CAN" CAN

A way for children to keep track of their new accomplishments.

You'll Need: soup or coffee cans, scrap materials or stickers, glue, scissors, drawing paper

Here's How: Have each child bring in a can to decorate. You may wish to mimeograph the words I CAN for them to glue onto the can. When a child learns something new or masters a skill, he should draw a picture or write a few lines about it on a piece of paper that will fit into the can. When it is complete, roll the paper into a scroll, date it, tie with ribbon or yarn, and place into the child's can. At the end of several months, children take the can home to share their progress with their parents.

SELF-PORTRAITS

Have the children draw themselves each month. Keep the pictures in their files. Their drawings often tell how they feel about themselves, as well as providing clues to their developmental progress.

You'll Need: crayons, markers, colored pencils, manila paper

Here's How: Ask each child to draw picture of himself. Do not remind him to add arms, legs, etc. As the child remembers to put more detail into his drawing, he is growing developmentally. Take some time to review pictures with the children to discuss changes and growth.

MY STARS

A way for the teacher to praise and encourage good work habits and skills.

You'll Need: construction paper, string or yarn, hole punch

Here's How: Cut a large star for each child in the class. When a child does something especially good, masters a skill, or just needs a bit of encouragement, put his name on the star. Write something about his accomplishment and hang the star from the ceiling or lights. Try for one star from each child.

FRIENDSHIP

A chance for children to discuss their friendships.

Here's How: Ask the children to explain how they know that someone is their friend. Record their responses. Ask the children if a person who is not their friend has ever acted or done things like the responses that they gave. Ask questions about how they make friends, characteristics of friends, and shared activities or interests. As a follow-up activity, the filmstrip "May I Bring a Friend?" by Weston Woods can be shown.

JOURNAL

A journal is an ideal way for young children to record their feelings, thoughts, perceptions, and fears.

You'll Need: small notebooks, pens or pencils

Here's How: Discuss the purpose of a journal, including the aspect of privacy. Set aside time each day for journal writing and encourage the children to write in their logs at any time. Let them know that you'll never correct their mechanics of writing or evaluate their entries.

MEMORIES

Students record the special events that occur during the year.

You'll Need: tape recorder and a supply of blank recording tapes

Here's How: Encourage children to share the special events that happen to them both in school and at home. Happenings may include a new sibling, news about their pets, visits from special relatives, or trips to special places. Tape each child as he reports his news to the class. At the end of the year, the children can relive some of their moments and share with the class the "update" of that event.

ALMANAC

Students can create their own personal almanac of information.

You'll Need: construction paper, drawing paper, pencils, markers

Here's How: Children should create their own scrapbook to be used to record personal information. Areas to be included would be important dates in their lives, school events in which they are involved, favorites such as: shows, foods, sports, and so on, lists of accomplishments and awards. A follow-up activity could be to explore other types of almanacs.

CLASS YEARBOOK

During the school year, assemble a scrapbook of material relating to the class.

You'll Need: one scrapbook with enough pages to hold a year's supply of papers and materials

Here's How: Make collections and samples during the year of art work, pictures, programs of special events, mementos of field trips, and so on. Encourage students to paste items into the book whenever they have things worth saving. At the end of the year, review the book as a class activity.

TEACHER'S BOOK OF CLASS RECORDS

Keep a record of the individual accomplishments of your students.

You'll Need: one piece of nine-by-twelve-inch cardboard for each student and bright, solid colored pieces of Contact paper large enough to cover the cardboard

Here's How: Have each child select his favorite color paper to cover his piece of cardboard. Have each student print his name across the top of the cardboard. Each student should select a place where he would like to place the board. Each board then becomes the student's own personal mini-bulletin board. Encourage the students to display papers, drawings, poems, etc.

STUDENT OF THE WEEK

This activity gives each child the opportunity to feel special and important for one week of school.

You'll Need: one shoebox brightly decorated and a card with every student's name printed on it.

Here's How: Place all the cards in the shoebox and be sure children know that their card is definitely in there. On Friday afternoon, draw one card at random from the box. That student becomes the student of the week for the following week. Have one bulletin board in the room reserved for the student of the week. The child may decorate the board with any personal pictures, posters, awards, banners, medals, etc. In the center of the board, place a list of special traits of the chosen student dictated by the other children. Special privileges may be granted to the student of the week such as being messenger, leading the flag salute, taking attendance, permission to skip one assignment, or selecting the game at gym time. At the end of the week, the student keeps the chart made by the class.

MIRROR, MIRROR

An activity for the young children that will allow them to feel good about their physical qualities.

You'll Need: a small hand mirror that can be passed around

Here's How: Have the children sit in a circle. One child at a time uses the mirror to look at himself. Ask the child to look in the mirror and pick out one thing that he sees that he likes about himself. Direct the children to give their answers in an "I like . . ." statement. If a child cannot think of anything, ask other students to help out. After everyone has a turn, talk about how they felt saying something nice about themselves in front of others.

SAME AND DIFFERENT

The children become aware of the likenesses and differences of others while developing an acceptance of both.

You'll Need: several sheets of oaktag, a scale, several yardsticks

Here's How: Divide the class into several small groups. Have the children weigh and measure each other. Place results onto the oaktag. Together, teacher and children form a composite sheet of the results. Discussion should center on the likenesses and differ‑ ences shown. Point out the advantages and disadvantages of each. Keep the atmosphere accepting of all differences to keep in the direction of the positive.

BABY FACE

Have the children become more aware of the changes and growth of their bodies.

You'll Need: two pictures of each child—one baby picture and one recent

Here's How: Divide a bulletin board into two parts. Place the baby pictures in random order on one side of the board. Place the current pictures on the other side. Ask the children to try to match the pictures. Discuss in a group how everyone has grown and the changes that have taken place. Added discussion can lead to social and emotional changes as well.

WRITE RIGHT

To develop the understanding of individual differences and an acceptance of the uniqueness of each child.

You'll Need: one three-by-five index card for each child, felt pens

Here's How: Pass out one card to each child. Instruct them to write the statement, I AM SPECIAL, on the card. They should not put their names on the cards. Collect all cards and place in random order on a table. Ask each child to pick out his own card by knowing his own writing. Discuss how each person's handwriting is unique. Develop an understanding of personal traits and characteristics that make each person different from the others. Discussion can lead to the special uniqueness of each child.

WHO CAN?—I CAN!

A bulletin board to point out the abilities of the students.

You'll Need: construction paper, medium-sized star pattern, markers

Here's How: Arrange on a bulletin board categories that are questions such as "Who can climb a tree?" "Who can read a whole book in one night?" "Who can swim across a pool without stopping?" "Who can skip rope?" etc. Try to have enough areas covered so that each child will be able to have at least one activity. Instruct children to make construction paper stars and to print their names across the center. Children then place their star(s) under the question that names an activity that they can do well. When the board is complete, have children share their accomplishments with one another. A follow-up could be to have children suggest other questions for the board.

GUESS WHO

A way to encourage listening skills and to appreciate the special qualities of others.

You'll Need: a tape recorder and blank tapes

Here's How: Set up an area in the room for recording. Allow each child to record some sentences about himself without giving his name. The sentences can be in the form of a riddle. When all the children have recorded, play the riddles one at a time for the entire class to hear. Have children guess the speaker's name by what was said and the voice tone. Encourage the children to listen carefully to others and to themselves.

TICKET GAME

A game that will boost relations and aid in following directions.

You'll Need: a pack of three-by-five index cards

Here's How: On the index cards, print directions to be followed. The directions on the cards should always be of a positive type. Examples: Tell us what makes you really happy; Shake hands with the person on your left; Tell us something nice about the person directly across from you; Tell us the thing that you do best; and so on. Have children sit in a circle. Each child selects a card from the pack and follows the directions exactly after he reads it first to the class. When the first child is finished, he gives the pack to the next child to draw from. Continue until all have a chance.

LISTENING CENTER (K-3rd)

An activity to help children explore emotions.

You'll Need: a tape recorder, blank tape, ditto sheet of happy, sad, angry faces

Here's How: Tape stories about children—someone who has lost their favorite toy, or whose pet or loved one has died, someone who has received their favorite present. Make sure children are able to identify with the story. Have the children listen to the story. Circle the face that shows how you think that person feels. (Older children may write about how the person feels.)

FINGERPRINTS (K-3rd)

We are all different. This activity makes children aware of subtle differences in our bodies.

You'll Need: finger paints or fingerprint ink, paper, cleaner

Here's How: Have the children make a print of their fingertips. Label the print. Compare the prints; point out the similarities and differences. See if the children can spot the differences in the prints. Fingerprints may later be used to make interesting designs or pictures.

WHAT IS IT?

An activity to help learn the location and names of various parts of the body.

You'll Need: flannel board, parts of the body cut from felt, labels made from cards backed with felt

Here's How:

1. Put the body together on the flannel board
2. Label the parts of the body
3. Check your answers with the answer sheet

The teacher should provide an answer sheet for the children with the parts of the body labeled correctly.

UNSPOKEN WORDS

To help children become aware of the messages we send without words. To help children understand that feelings can be communicated through facial expressions.

You'll Need: pictures of faces showing various expressions, mirror, paper, crayons

Here's How: Look at the groups of faces. Ask the children "How do you think the faces are alike?" "What do you think the faces are saying?" Have the children take a piece of paper and draw faces showing different feelings. They can look in the mirror to help them draw the faces.

BODY AWARENESS

To encourage body awareness through measurement.

You'll Need: A ditto of the list that follows, pencils, tape measure, ruler, yardstick

Feet _____   Height _____
Hands _____   Weight _____
Arms _____
Legs _____
Whose arms/legs are longest? _____
Who weighs the most? _____
Who weighs the least? _____
Who is taller? _____

Here's How: Find a partner. With your partner, measure the things listed and answer the questions on the sheet. Duplicate a list with everyone's names on it. Use it to focus on body awareness.

BODY MEASUREMENT

Using various parts of the body as a measuring device.

You'll Need: ruler, tape measure, yardstick (can be done with metrics)

Here's How: Find a partner. With your partner, use your hand or some part of your body to measure the length of these distances. Other distances may be added.

> The distance from the fish tank to the front door
> The length of your desk
> The width of your math book
> The height of the reading table, etc.

AUTOBIOGRAPHY

An activity to make children aware of the differences in our voices. The activity also helps children to get to know each other.

You'll Need: a tape recorder and blank tape

Here's How: Use the tape recorder. Tell us about yourself. *Do not* give your name until you are finished. Tell us:

What you look like
Where you live
How you feel today
About things you like
About things you don't like
About your family

You may tell us these things in any order. You may include any other information you would like to share.

At the end of the day play one tape that was recorded. Have children try to guess who recorded it. Some may be able to tell by voice. Discuss the uniqueness of each voice.

WHAT DO YOU SEE?

Children become aware of themselves and others through this activity.

You'll Need: flannel board, flannel board shapes (Flannel board shapes: round, oval, heart-shaped, square; flannel board colors: brown, white, pink, tan, black, orange, red), mirror

Here's How: Look in the mirror. Choose the shape you see. Make your face on the flannel board.

MOVABLE DOLL PEOPLE

An activity to make children aware of body parts and body movement.

You'll Need: construction paper or oaktag, pencil and crayons, scissors, brass fasteners, scrap box

Here's How: Draw the parts of you that move. Cut them out. Connect the parts where they move with fasteners. Your result will be a movable doll.

Children decide how many movable parts they want to make. May be done with partners. Use dolls in role-playing.

WHAT DO I LIKE TO DO?

To help children increase their self-understanding and to help children get to know each other.

You'll Need: happy and sad face, cards with children doing and participating in different activities

Here's How:

1. Have the children take picture cards.
2. Ask the children, "What are the children doing?"
3. Have the children put the card under the happy face if they like what the children are doing or put the card under the sad face if they dislike what the children are doing.
4. Compile a list of all the children's likes.

Teachers may set up a bulletin board or learning center with a place for the children to hang the activity cards. Younger children may draw pictures of their likes.

FAMILY TREE

To give each child a sense of belonging. This is especially good to use at the beginning of the school year.

I
am Bill.
I like
baseball.

You'll Need: leaf patterns, construction paper, hole punch, yarn, and tree branch

Here's How: Give each child a colored leaf. Older children can trace and cut their own from patterns. Staple the tree branch to your bulletin board or place it in a bucket of sand. Ask the class to sit around the family tree as each child brings his leaf to you. Print the child's name on the leaf (older children can do their own), punch a hole in it, and tie yarn. Ask each child to tell you something about himself. Write it on the leaf (older children can do their own) and let the child hang his leaf on the tree.

OPEN UP

To help the children get in touch with their feelings.

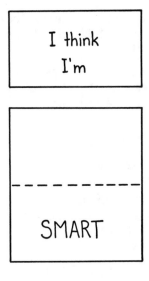

You'll Need: scissors, construction paper, glue or paste, and ditto with the following:

> My friends think I'm ...
> My teacher thinks I'm ...
> My Mom thinks I'm ...
> My Dad thinks I'm ...
> I think I'm ...

Here's How: Cut the phrases apart or have the children do it themselves. Give each child five five-by-seven-inch pieces of construction paper to fold in half. Have the children glue one phrase on the front of each piece of folded construction paper. Have the children dictate or write the answer to the phrase on the inside.

WHISPER BOX

Use a large carton to make a quiet place to sit and think.

You'll Need: a large cardboard box, scissors, material scraps, wallpaper, glue

Here's How: Cut a hole in the box so that the children may whisper through it. Encourage the children to decorate the "Whisper Box" with material and wallpaper.

One child sits inside the box and whispers through the hole to another child or the teacher sitting outside. If the teacher or an aide listens, keep a record of the children's thoughts and wishes.

I AM SPECIAL STAMPS

If you are very busy this year helping children feel special, here's a time-saving idea. From a stationery or an office supply store, purchase a stamp that reads: I AM SPECIAL. The children can then make their own badges and other projects. Other stamp ideas are: HOORAY FOR ME, I'M GLAD I'M ME, I LIKE ME.

SNOW KIDS

Change the traditional snowman and make it more meaningful to the children.

You'll Need: white construction paper, circles (large, medium, small), glue, crayons, photograph of each child

Here's How: Give each child the three circle shapes needed to make his snow kid. Have them give the snow kids a hat, scarf, broom, etc. Do not have them draw in the faces. Cut the child's face from his snapshot and have him glue it where the face should be on the snow kid.

THE HAPPY/SAD/ANGRY BOX

Get the children to talk about the things that make them happy, sad, or angry.

You'll Need: three shoeboxes, Contact paper, colored circles, crayons

Here's How: Cover the three shoeboxes with Contact paper. Give each child three circles and ask him to draw a happy face, a sad face, and an angry face. Collect circles and place happy, sad and angry circles in each shoebox. Divide the class into three groups.

Each child closes his eyes and draws a circle from the box. He then names the feeling expressed by the face and tells something that makes him happy, sad, or angry.

NAME GAME

This provides an opportunity for each student to express individual characteristics and personality traits.

You'll Need: construction paper, markers, crayons

Here's How: Have each child spell his name vertically down the left side of the paper. Next to each letter, have the child write a word or phrase beginning with that letter to describe himself. Once all name banners are completed, they should be displayed around the room. Examples:

F — fast runner		J — jumps around
R — reader		A — argues
A — adds quickly		M — Mom's helper
N — nice to others		E — eats a lot
K — keeps desk neat		S — smiles often

EMOTION SCRAPBOOK

Have students become more aware and accepting of their feelings.

You'll Need: paper, crayons, scissors, paste, old magazines

Here's How: Have each child make a scrapbook of his feelings. Head each page with a word such as happy, afraid, angry, proud, etc. On the page, each student draws pictures or pastes magazine pictures that depict a feeling in a personal way. Have a sharing time so that children can see that their peers may be experiencing the same emotions they are. Some can be encouraged to write a story about when and why they had these feelings.

PICTURE THIS

This activity encourages beginning reading skills while you get to know each student on a personal level.

You'll Need: a composite class picture or individual pictures of each child, bulletin board space, pushpins, construction paper

Here's How: Prepare sentences about class members or children in general. Try to use a variety of sentence forms. Write out each sentence on a separate piece of colored construction paper. Post several sentences at the beginning of each week in the center of the bulletin board with children's pictures around it. As children are able to read and comprehend the sentence, they place their picture next to the sentence if it applies to themselves. At week's end, select children to read their sentences. Examples:

> I have a big brother.
> I am a good helper in our class.
> She has a tooth missing.
> Who is a good worker?

BIRTHDAY TREAT

To encourage personal creativity and examine personal feelings and interests.

You'll Need: large drawing paper, crayons, pencils

Here's How: Gather the class together in a circle for discussion. Center on birthdays and parties. Each child should suggest ideas for having an ideal party or celebration in honor of his birthday. After the discussion, provide paper, pencils, and crayons. Each child draws a picture of his ideal birthday party. Explain that there will be no restrictions, such as cost or the number of people involved. On the back of the drawing, the child writes an explanation of what makes his party special or different. Older children can also suggest a guest list, menu, games, location, and so on. Provide a sharing time to examine the pictures and stories.

FEELINGS

Students learn to understand and recognize the many different feelings that we experience.

You'll Need: three-by-five blank index cards, pencils

Here's How: Have each child list on the index card three ways he felt during the past week (happy, sad, alone, angry). Collect all of the cards. The teacher selects one card at a time and reads the feelings to the class. Suggestions:

1. Have the children show how their faces would look for that feeling.
2. Have one or two children explain when and why they also felt that way.
3. Have one or two children act out their emotions.
4. Find pictures in old magazines that show these feelings.

Role-play situations that could cause those feelings.

CLASS TREE

Have the children trace their hands and then use them to make a class tree.

You'll Need: construction paper, pencils, scissors, crayons

Here's How: Have each child trace his hand on construction paper. Use colors suitable for fall colors. Have the children cut out their hands and write their names on them with crayon. Attach the hands to the shape of a tree on the bulletin board. This is a good way to get to know one another in September.

MY SCHOOL DAY

This activity is good for "Back to School Night." This activity will help the parents become aware of some of their child's interests in school.

You'll Need: composition or story paper, pencils, drawing paper, construction paper, crayons, yarn, hole punch or stapler

Here's How: Help the children compile a booklet entitled, *My School Day.* Younger children may draw a series of pictures of themselves during the school day. The teacher should label the pictures in the child's own words. Older children may write short paragraphs or stories about their school day. They may illustrate their stories as they wish.

This activity may be done by the whole group or at a center. The booklet should be compiled over the period of at least a week so that the children have ample time to complete the project without feeling pressured. When the booklets are completed, they can be stapled together with a cover made by the child or they can be tied together with colorful yarn.

MY ROOM

The children create signs for their rooms, making them special places.

You'll Need: pre-cut letters, wallpaper books, glue, clear Contact paper

Here's How: The children choose pieces of wallpaper that go with the colors of their rooms at home. Give them the letters of their names and letters that spell ROOM. Help them glue the letters to the strip of wallpaper. Cover the signs with clear Contact paper. Ask the children where they will hang their signs. Older children can trace and cut out their own letters.

WHAT I'D LIKE TO BE

Have the children write about, draw pictures of, or act out their future ambitions or desires. It doesn't have to be when they grow up—it could be next month, next year, in junior or senior high school—let the children decide.

SECURITY BLANKETS

Have the children create their own "Security Blankets."

You'll Need: clothesline, old pieces of sheets, markers

Here's How: Give each child a piece of an old sheet. Have each child think of something that makes him happy and draw a picture of it on the sheet with marker. Hang a piece of clothesline from one corner of the room to another, and when the "blankets" are finished, hang each one on the clothesline for all to see.

BIRTHDAY SURPRISE

Surprise the children who have summer birthdays by preparing birthday packets to be opened on their birthdays.

You'll Need: construction paper, used greeting cards, stickers, stapler, glue

Here's How: Make each summer birthday child an envelope by stapling two nine-by-twelve-inch pieces of construction paper together, leaving the top open. Have the class create birthday cards with used greeting cards and folded construction paper. Some fun worksheets, matching games, homemade books, etc. can be added to the birthday packets. Add a tag to each envelope that says, "Do not open until _____. HAPPY BIRTHDAY FROM YOUR FRIENDS." child's birthdate

RECOGNITION CLASSO

This is a good game for the beginning of the school year that helps the children get to know one another.

You'll Need: five-by-eight index cards, pencils, colored paper, markers

Here's How: Mark off the index cards so that they have 25 boxes. Put your name in the middle box. Pass out the cards and have the children go around and fill in their cards with the names of their classmates. Next, pass out markers and play "Classo." You merely put all of the names in a hat or box and call one out at a time. Or you can call out identifying features of each person such as: the girl with the curly brown hair. The children locate each person and mark his or her name on their cards. Keep playing until someone has marked five names in a row.

"I DID SOMETHING NICE" BULLETIN BOARD

This board helps stimulate good feelings about oneself and good relationship among your students.

You'll Need: bulletin board with caption "I Did Something Nice for Someone Today"

Here's How: Two or three days a week have the children tell what other children in the class did to help them. Don't let the children know exactly what day you will be asking this question. Write the name of the helper and the child helped on a seasonally shaped piece of paper (such as leaves for September) and staple them to the board. Keep a record of how many times each child's name appears as a helper. At the end of the month, the child who helped others the most wins a photo of himself and those he helped.

MANNERS MATTER MONTH

Young children need to develop positive attitudes toward others, and those who do have a more positive attitude toward themselves. Using the theme of "Manners Matter Month," children can be helped to explore their feelings toward others and their relationships with their peers.

Here's How: Young children could develop their ideas through art and role-playing. Some examples of areas to be explored follow:

How do you feel when someone pulls your toy away?
What is the polite thing to do when this happens?
Johnny has a stack of things in his hands . . . . should you offer to help or hold the door?
Why should you say please and thank you?

Teachers can create many situations for children to react to. Older children may prefer to write about their feelings. Manners booklets can be made and illustrated. Murals can be drawn. Use your imagination to help the children discover how manners affect their relationships with others.

HOLIDAY ACTIVITIES

THANKSGIVING

Thanksgiving Feast: The idea of friendship and sharing can be fostered through this activity.

Here's How: Help the children plan and prepare a small "Thanksgiving Feast." Working in small groups to plan and make decorations, the menu, and the food will help the children become aware of the importance of everyone working as a team to make the feast a success. It will also help the children become aware of their feelings and those of others.

CHRISTMAS AND HANUKKAH

Christmas and Hanukkah Celebrations: Christmas (or Hanukkah) is a good time to make children aware of their own heritages. A study of how holidays are celebrated by various ethnic groups helps the children to understand the cultures of others.

Here's How: Stories, poems, and visits from parents help to explain the various observances. Older children may also research some of the holiday observances. Each day in the month of December can be used to learn about a different culture. Be sure to start with the cultural backgrounds in your class first. The depth of your study will depend on your class. Simple holiday foods may also be prepared and bulletin boards set up. Children enjoy learning about themselves and their families.

A Wreath of Hands: A wreath made of cutouts of children's hands adds a special meaning to the holidays.

You'll Need: green construction paper, scissors, stapler, large piece of oaktag, red bow

Here's How: Cut a large doughnut shape from the oaktag. Give each child a piece of green construction paper and have them trace around their hands as many times as they can. Have them cut out their hands. Curl the fingers by wrapping them around a pencil. Staple the hands around the wreath frame. Add a bow.

THE NEW YEAR

Happy New Year Specials: Here's a bulletin board that makes the New Year extra special.

You'll Need: colored balloons, paper

Here's How: Write each child's name on a small piece of paper. Roll the paper and place it inside a balloon. Ask the children to blow up the balloons. Pin them on the bulletin board that says HAPPY NEW YEAR. Each day break one balloon. The child whose name is inside becomes the special child of the day. He may wear a special badge or medal that day. After a child's balloon has been popped, replace his balloon with his picture.

Resolutions: The start of the year is also a good time to take a look at ourselves. The children can write or draw "Things About Me I Like" and "Things About Me I Would Like to Change or Improve." The stories or pictures can be displayed on a bulletin board.

VALENTINES' DAY

Valentine Bulletin Board: A loving bulletin board from your class.

LOVE IS...

ROOM
9

You'll Need: red and white construction paper, scissors, marker, stapler

Here's How: Use either red or white construction paper to back your bulletin board. Trace each child's hands on the contrasting color construction paper. Older children can do their own. Cut out hands. Place the hands on the bulletin board in the shape of a heart. Attach with a stapler. Add letters to say LOVE IS . . . The children can then be asked to tell what they think love is and these can be written around the heart with a marker.

ST. PATRICK'S DAY

Make a Pot of Gold to help you select the "Children of the Day."

You'll Need: black, gold, green, white construction paper, scissors, stapler

Here's How: With the black construction paper, cut a pot of gold. Staple the edges and bottom to the bulletin board, leaving the top open. Cut out green and white shamrocks, and write each child's name on one shamrock. Place the names in the "Pot of Gold." Each day draw two names from the pot—a Lassie and a Laddie. These children will be the "Extra Special" children for that day.

IRISH SWEEPSTAKES BULLETIN BOARD

This is an exciting bulletin board that will give each child a thrill of winning and being the "Child of the Day."

You'll Need: shamrock patterns, stapler, markers, gold candy coins, pot of gold, paint or crayons.

Here's How: Obtain a plastic pot or create one from construction paper. Place the pot of gold under a rainbow painted or colored by the children. Fill the pot with the candy coins. Have the children trace and cut out two small shamrocks and staple them together at the top so that one can be lifted up. Write the child's name inside. Place the shamrocks on the board so that the children do not know where their shamrock is. Each day select the sweepstakes winner by lifting up the top of one of the shamrocks. Tear the top shamrock off and pin it to the "Child of the Day." That child receives a coin from the pot of gold.

EASTER

"Good Egg" Easter Eggs: Here's a bulletin board that combines an Easter activity with choosing a special "Child of the Day."

You'll Need: construction paper ovals, crayons, hole punch, yarn, stapler, Easter basket made from construction paper or wallpaper

Here's How: The teacher makes an Easter basket for the board. Many wallpaper books have basket weave patterns that make excellent baskets. Staple the basket to the board.

Have the children design an Easter egg, punch a hole through the top, and thread yarn through the hole. Write each child's name on his egg. Put all the eggs in the basket. Each day choose a "Good Egg" for the day. That child wears his egg to signify that he's the "Good Egg" for the day.

6

Activities in the Creative Arts

The activities in this chapter are divided into the areas of art, movement and music, and cooking. An ideal way to reinforce a child's self-concept is to have him create an original design, dance, or simple dessert that can express his individuality. The feeling of accomplishment and the pride in having done something that is uniquely his own will contribute to his positive feelings of self-worth and value. Children who may experience learning difficulties in the academic areas often find in the creative arts areas special ways to express themselves more fully. The final creation, whether it is a drawing, dance sequence, or food dish, should be accepted as praiseworthy and a job well done.

The activities as presented in this chapter are not meant to be followed exactly, but rather as starting points, to be adapted and adjusted to fit the needs of individual classes. Adding to these activities can be a source of added pride and accomplishment for the children. Allow a sharing time to follow each activity during which the children have the opportunity to present their creations to the class as a whole. The sense of pride, accomplishment, and acceptance that they will experience can foster a good self-image.

ME COLLAGE

To allow each child to display his interests, hobbies, goals, etc. for the class to share.

You'll Need: large sheet of white paper, old magazines, paste, and scissors

Here's How: Have the children search through magazines looking for pictures that describe themselves. Includes likes, interests, hobbies, actions, goals, and feelings. When enough pictures are cut out, arrange them on the paper in the form of a collage. Allow a sharing time for each child to explain his choice of pictures, then display the collages as a class project.

VESTED INTERESTS

To create an individual profile of the interests and concerns of the children.

You'll Need: an old shirt or vest for each child, old magazines, pictures, pins, glue, tape, and scissors

Here's How: Designate one day to explore individual interests and concerns. Children discuss and explore hobbies, likes and dislikes, goals, skills, and so on. Have the children look through magazines for pictures or symbols that represent their ideas. Glue, pin, or tape them to the vest or shirt. Allow a sharing time for each child to model his creation and to discuss the significance of the pictures or symbols as they relate to him personally.

SMILE, SMILE, SMILE

To encourage children to make positive statements about their peers in a creative manner.

You'll Need: construction paper, circle patterns, markers, and scissors

Here's How: Cut out six-inch smile faces out of various colors of construction paper. Leave a space on each for printing a short sentence. Each child receives one smile face to draw and decorate. On the face they record one positive statement about another child in the class. When all are completed, each child stands up, reads his statement and then presents the smile face to that person. Faces can be worn, placed on the bulletin board, or displayed on desks.

TOUCH AND GO

To foster an interest in and an appreciation of the individual differences among classmates.

You'll Need: ink pad, paper, and tape recorder

Here's How: Have each child make prints of their fingers on the top of a paper. Underneath the prints, the child prints some identification data. Include height, weight, eye color, freckles, etc. When papers are completed, each child records his information on tape. The class examines the prints. Stress the differences in prints and voice patterns—high, low, fast, slow, accents, and so on. Encourage children to see that while they all have much in common, they are unique as individuals.

DANDY CANDY

To have students express feelings about themselves in a positive manner.

You'll Need: colored construction paper, cut in three-by-nine-inch portions, and crayons

Here's How: Have each child pretend he is a candy bar. Children are to create the wrapper for the candy bar on one side of the construction paper. Be sure to include the name, weight, price, and so on. On the reverse side have children list the ingredients of the candy bar that proves it's really them. Example: freckles, curly hair, bright smile, helpful attitude, etc.

BODY BEAUTIFUL

To have children become more aware of their physical characteristics in a fun and creative way.

You'll Need: large-size brown mural paper, crayons, markers, and scissors

Here's How: By random selection, one child each day is chosen to lie down on mural paper to be traced by a classmate. Each child colors in his outline portrait, keeping in mind specific body characteristics. On the outline shape, record personal data—age, birthdate, phone number, likes and dislikes, hobbies, and goals. Display portraits around the classroom.

BAGGIES

To help children think and talk about themselves in an accepting atmosphere.

You'll Need: several small mirrors, small brown lunch bags (one for each child), crayons, and markers

Here's How: Have each child examine his face using and sharing the mirrors. Then have each try to draw his face on the bag including as many traits as possible for identification. Suggest freckles, curly hair, glasses, bright smile, or missing teeth. Completed bags can be displayed on a bulletin board and invite class visitors to guess who's who. Bags can also be used as hand puppets to act out classroom situations or for role-playing.

INITIAL PENNANTS

To have children create and design individual pennants for classroom display.

You'll Need: construction paper, scrap material, vinyl stick-on letters, and old magazines

Here's How: Give each child a triangular shape of construction paper. Each child places his initials on the center of the pennant. Have them decorate the pennant with scrap material cut-outs, pictures, or original drawings. Display finished creations around the room and allow a sharing time for each child to present his to the class.

ME MOBILE

Each child creates a free-hanging mobile that depicts his personality.

You'll Need: magazine pictures, scissors, clothes hangers, hole punch, and yarn

Here's How: Have the children search through old magazines for pictures or symbols that describe themselves. Let the children draw and cut out original pictures as well. Punch holes through the pictures and drawings. Thread the yarn through and attach to wire coat hangers. Display the mobiles around the room.

BALLOON WISHES WEEK

To encourage children to express their thoughts and wishes in an open and supportive atmosphere.

You'll Need: colored balloons, strips of paper, pencils, yarn, and markers

Here's How: Have each child select a balloon. Each child writes on a strip of paper his secret wish about himself, family, or friends. Place the wishes inside the balloon and inflate. Have the children decorate their balloon and then attach a length of yarn and hang around the room. Select one child each day to select a balloon, break it, and read aloud the wish. Allow time for class discussion and follow-up activities.

IN MY HEAD

To have children express their thoughts, dreams, and personal ideas in a fun and creative manner.

You'll Need: silhouettes of each child, magazines, paste, scissors, markers, crayons, and construction paper

Here's How: Hold a discussion with the children about the things they like to think or daydream about. Have children make collages of their thoughts. Paste the silhouette of each child in the middle of the piece of construction paper. All around the silhouette have the children draw or paste pictures of the things going on in their heads.

CHARACTERISTIC SELF-PORTRAITS

To give each child the chance to express his personality and physical traits.

You'll Need: heavy brown paper in large sheets, pencils, crayons, and scissors

Here's How: Divide the children into pairs. Have children trace one another's body outline on the heavy brown paper. Have children cut out and write their names across the middle in big letters. Discuss with the children a list of short sentences that describe themselves. Include physical characteristics, likes and dislikes, skills, strengths, wishes, and goals. Have the children record their sentences on their life-size portraits.

HAPPY, SAD, SILLY, MAD

The children explore their feelings and then create a collage to express them.

You'll Need: large sheets of oaktag or construction paper, magazines, glue, scissors, markers, and the book *Happy, Sad, Silly, Mad* by Barbara Shook Hazen

Here's How: Read the Hazen book to the class. Create a large chart of the four emotions expressed in the title. Have children design and cut out a face to represent the four feelings. Place the faces at the top of the chart. Have children search through magazines and cut out pictures of faces that show these feelings. Paste or glue the pictures in their appropriate places. As the children select their pictures, discuss when and why they have felt these feelings. Then discuss the pictures selected.

PEOPLE PENDANTS

To create a gift that will help children take pride in themselves.

You'll Need: small jar lids, photographs of each child or pictures they have drawn, yarn or braid, construction paper, felt scraps, and hole punch

Here's How: Have the children trace two felt circles using the jar lid as a pattern. The circles should be glued to the top and the inside of the jar lid. Glue to the inside the picture of the child or decorate with an original design. Have the child decorate the edges of the lid with yarn or braid. When the lids are complete, punch a hole in the lid and thread with yarn or ribbon.

FAMILY SHIELD

To encourage an interest in and pride about family life and personal views.

You'll Need: crayons, markers, pencils, and a ditto of a blank shield

Here's How: Have the children create their own family shield by filling in the areas of the crest. Suggested items are pictures of family members, scenes of activities the family does together, pictures of places visited, pictures of their home, pets, and relatives. Allow a sharing time for each child to present his shield to the class and discuss its contents.

SELF-PORTRAITS

To discover the way in which the children view themselves and to encourage awareness of the likes and differences of individuals.

You'll Need: white drawing paper, crayons or markers

Here's How: Starting with the first month of school, have the children draw their self-portraits at the end of each month. Over the months watch for changes and signs of growth and development. Keep all the pictures and compare as time goes on, looking for improvements in drawing skills as well. On the back of each picture, have the children record several short sentences that tell how they have changed, grown, or developed from the last picture. Include new skills learned, goals reached, changes in attitudes or behavior, and so on.

ME DOLLS

To have each child design and create his own doll that shows his individuality.

You'll Need: brown craft or wrapping paper, markers, scissors, and paint

Here's How: Have the children work in pairs. Each takes a turn tracing the body outline of his partner. Have them cut out the tracing of their body. Have each child paint or color in his face. Ask the children to bring in a set of old clothes so that they can dress their dolls. If they cannot bring in the clothes, the children can paint the doll figures to correspond to one of their outfits. Finished creations can be displayed on walls or around the room. Children may even enjoy taking their portraits "on parade" to other classes.

SILHOUETTES

To encourage an interest in and an awareness of the individual differences of class members.

You'll Need: overhead projector or powerful flashlight, dark construction paper

Here's How: Tape the piece of construction paper to the blackboard or a wall. Use the projector or flashlight to throw the silhouette of the child's profile as he stands between the light and the paper. Trace the profile onto the dark colored paper. Display the pictures around the room and allow a time for guessing who's who. When correct identifications have been made, discuss how they recognized each individual.

CRYSTAL BALLS

Children have the opportunity to express their hopes, goals, and dreams of the future.

You'll Need: construction paper cut into circles, markers, and crayons

Here's How: Give each child four of the circles of various colors. Each circle represents an amount of time in the future. In each circle the child draws a picture of what he expects to be like at that time. Suggestions—next year, in five years, ten years, and fifteen. When time circles are completed, have them mounted on large sheets of construction paper. Allow a sharing time for each child to explain what his "Crystal Ball" circles predict for his future.

FRIENDSHIPS

To encourage children to discuss their choice of friends and to discuss the meaning of friendships.

You'll Need: construction paper folded in thirds by length, pencils, and markers

Here's How. Have each child draw his three best friends in the areas of the construction paper. Underneath each drawing the child writes a few short sentences to explain why this person is his friend. Allow a sharing time for each child to present his pictures. Discuss how people become friends, what responsibilities a friend has, what we can learn about a person by learning about his friends. Encourage responses about growth and changes in the relationships during the year at school.

NEEDLEPOINT INITIALS

To offer the children an opportunity to express their individuality by creating their own needlepoint design of their initials.

You'll Need: needlepoint canvas with large holes cut into eight-by-eleven-inch pieces, yarn, and needles.

Here's How: On a piece of canvas, have the child use his initials to create a design. Have the children use two colors of yarn to fill in their initial designs on the canvas. Display finished designs around the room or on desks.

PICTURE THIS

To foster an interest in the individuality and personal interests of the class.

You'll Need: pictures of each child, poster paper, old magazines, and scissors

Here's How: Have each child bring in two pictures of himself—one baby photo and one recent. Have the children fold the poster paper in half. Mount the baby picture on one side and the recent picture on the other. Using the old magazines, have children search for both pictures and words that describe themselves at these two times. Children should cut out and mount the words and pictures that they have selected next to the appropriate picture. Allow for a sharing time for each child to present his poster to the class. Discuss the differences evident between the two sides of the poster and encourage the children to discuss their growth and development.

BLOOM AND GROW

To create a bulletin board that features the children of the class.

You'll Need: corrugated colored cardboard, scissors, construction paper, and tissue paper

Here's How: Have the children make large flower petals from the corrugated cardboard. Have the children arrange the petals into a flower shape, leaving the circle in the center blank. Have the children put a small snapshot of themselves in the center. If no pictures are handy, have them draw the picture. Arrange the flowers on a bulletin board "garden," adding stems and smaller tissue paper flowers to border the display.

MY WORLD

The children will make a mural of their neighborhood.

You'll Need: construction paper, crayons, glue, scissors, mural paper

Here's How: Have each child design and cut out a model of his house. Be sure to encourage them to include as many details as possible for identification. Each child glues his house onto the neighborhood mural. The mural can be mapped into streets, landmarks, and the school. As a follow-up, teach the song "My Street Begins at My House" from the Ella Jenkins record of the same name. Plan a walking tour of the neighborhood.

PANTOMIME PAIRS

To enhance the awareness of feelings and expressions of others.

You'll Need: slips of paper with a feeling word printed on each (suggested list: anger, surprise, joy, fear, bashful, excited, lonely, curious, etc.)

Here's How: Have the children form pairs and select an area of the room to work. Each child takes a turn at randomly selecting a slip of paper. Then the child pantomimes or acts out that emotion. The partner tries to guess the feeling word. Have the pairs discuss and describe how they recognized the words.

PANTOMIME—WHO AM I?

This activity enables the children to understand how the body and face can show emotions and feelings.

You'll Need: A listing of people who can be identified by their actions, stance, or demeanor. Suggested list: soldier, ballet dancer, king or queen, clown, monster, tired child, and so on.

Here's How: Have the children read this listing of various people. Discuss how each one acts, feels, looks, and behaves. Select one child to become one of the people and then pantomime or act out that person. The other children guess which person on the list has been selected. Discuss the clues and ideas that led to the proper identification.

PANTOMIME—FEELINGS

This activity shows the children how facial expressions and body movements can show mood or emotion.

You'll Need: a list of sentences that depict situations suggesting certain emotions (sample sentences: A great big dog is chasing you down the street. Someone just wrote all over your favorite book. You lost your favorite toy. You have won first prize in a contest.)

Here's How: Arrange the children into a circle. Have one child select one of the sentences and read it silently. Then the child pantomimes or acts out the situation or emotion indicated by the sentence. The other children try to guess which feeling or emotion has been selected. Discuss the clues and ideas that led to the correct response. Have the child who correctly named the feeling become the next mime.

LIGHT UP MY LIFE

The children have the opportunity to express their thoughts and feelings about the important people in their lives.

You'll Need: a recording of the song "You Light Up My Life," construction paper, scissors, and markers

Here's How: Have children listen to the record. Discuss what the words mean to them. Encourage them to suggest people in their own lives that have a direct influence upon them. Have the children design, color, and cut out the shape of a candle and flame. On the flame, have them print the name of the person that they feel lights up their life. On the candle itself, have them write a short sentence telling why they chose that person. Allow for a sharing time for each to present his candle to the group before displaying.

SHADOW ACTS

Children become more aware of the actions and uniqueness of their peers.

You'll Need: a length of rope to stretch across the room, an overhead projector or powerful flashlight, sheet or other large white cloth

Here's How: Stretch the length of rope across the room. Hang the material over the rope, making a curtain. Place the light source behind the material, shining upon it. The performer stands between the light and the curtain so that he casts his shadow on it. Have the children sit in front of the curtain. Have them close their eyes while you select one or two to perform. The child selected should act out motions behind the curtain while the others try to identify them. Suggest that they act out doing their favorite sport or hobby. Ideas: swinging a bat, shooting baskets, dancing, painting a picture. When the correct identification has been made, discuss the responses and clues.

ANIMAL ACTS

The children become more aware of body movement and music.

You'll Need: a copy of the recording "Carnival of the Animals," record player

Here's How: Instruct the children to listen carefully to the music as each animal is mentioned. After the initial playing, repeat and allow the children to move about, pretending to be any of the animals (lions, turtles, kangaroo, elephant, donkey). As a follow-up, have children listen to and learn:

I've acted like the animals
from the carnival and zoo,
I've walked so slowly like the turtle
and hopped like the kangaroo.
But of all the animals I've tried to be
The one I think I like the best is—
Me! Me! Me!

MOVEMENT AND FEELINGS

To have the children act out and express emotions and discuss reactions.

You'll Need: a large area of space in which the children may move about freely

Here's How: Discuss how feelings are often expressed through movement. Ask the children if they have ever been able to tell if someone was angry just by the way that he walked. Explain that you are going to describe situations and the children will take turns imagining how they would feel in that situation. They then will act out or express through motions only their feelings. Have children notice how each person expresses feelings differently. Do some children have stronger feelings and reactions than others? Repeat the same situation with several children so that comparisons can be made. Examples:

1. You just found out that your brother or sister broke your favorite toy.
2. You are walking into a new class in a new school.
3. You just received a poor report card and you are walking home to show it to your parents.
4. It is the first really nice day of spring and you are on your way to meet your friends for a picnic.
5. You are walking alone and you see a very big mean-looking dog coming toward you.

MOVEMENT—ALIVE

The children act out the cycle of seedling to sprout to flower using music.

You'll Need: a recording of Richard Wagner's "Tristan und Isolde, Liebestodt," record player

Here's How: Allow the children as much freedom for movement as your space permits. Begin by listening to the music and ask the children how they feel they should move to the music. Read the poem "Alive" slowly and end as the music peaks.

ALIVE!

You are a tiny seed, curled up beneath the deep, dark soft brown earth.
The days have been so cold—no warm sunlight has reached you for many days.
Then one day, there is a strange feeling around you.
The sun is shining and its bright orange beams touch you.
Oh! That feels good. You tingle all over!
You begin pushing your sprouts up through the ground.
Slowly, slowly, you grow—stretching, stretching, pushing, pushing—
Until the sun touches you!
Your leaves begin to spread—a beautiful bud is opening.
Rain falls upon your face and one day a flower blooms.
And now you know you are beautiful and it's good to be Alive!

During the reading of the poem, have the children imitate the motions that are suggested by the words of the poem. For example: children start out all curled up on the floor, then there is very slight body movement, then hands and arms push upward, the arms spread out slowly, the head lifts upward and by the end, arms spread wide and stretch out high.

MOVEMENT—THE BUTTERFLY

Through simple body movements, the children act out the cycle of the changes from caterpillars to butterflies using music.

You'll Need: a recording of Edward Grieg's "Peer Gynt Lyric Suite," a record player

Here's How: Have the children listen carefully to the music, keeping in mind the motions or actions suggested by the music. Allow the children to move freely to express these movements. Read the poem "The Butterfly" as the music plays and the children move.

THE BUTTERFLY

You are a tiny egg resting on a soft green leaf.
A beautiful butterfly left you there. Make your body round
and small so that you are like the egg.

After some time the little eggs begin to open. And do you
know what's inside? Why they're yellow and black
caterpillars! Show me how a caterpillar moves on
his stomach. Can you wiggle too?

Now the caterpillars are hungry. They eat tiny leaves and
now they are fat and tired. Crawl out on your leaf,
little caterpillars. Now you'll hang yourself upside
down like the letter J.

Now sleep, little caterpillars, sleep. Curl up tightly,
make yourself very small inside the new home you have
spun around yourself. Sleep.

As the little caterpillars sleep their bodies are changing.
They stay inside their chrysalis for a long time until
the day the chrysalis opens and the little caterpillars
are gone—inside, spreading wings to dry are beautiful
butterflies. Dry your wings, butterflies, and fly away!

Have the children take turns giving their interpretation of the
changing music and motions. Allow a sharing time for discussion of
the ways the children have seen real caterpillars and butterflies
move about. Encourage them to move about freely in order to
express their thoughts and feelings. As a follow-up activity, you
may wish to create a bulletin board depicting the life cycle of the
butterfly. Children could design and color pictures of the various
stages they acted out to the music and story.

KIDS IN THE KITCHEN

MACARONI NAMES

You'll Need: alphabet macaroni, construction paper, glue

Here's How: Give each child one-half cup of alphabet macaroni.
Have them search for the letters in their names. Arrange the letters
on the construction paper and then glue into place. For the older

children, have them look for letters to spell out a few adjectives to describe themselves. Letter designs can also be painted on the paper to add color to the creation.

APPLE ME

You'll Need: apples, table knife, lemon juice, and mirrors

Here's How: Peel large cooking apples and then, using a table knife, the teacher helps each child cut deep slices for his facial features. Make shallow slits for wrinkles—these will deepen as the apple dries. Soak the fruit in lemon juice for an hour and set in a warm, airy place to dry. Drying takes about four to six weeks. Rouge can then be applied for cheek color.

AGGRESSION COOKIES

You'll Need: three cups of oatmeal, one and one half cups of brown sugar, one and one half cups of flour, one and one half cups of butter, and one and one half teaspoons of baking powder.

Here's How: Have children dump everything into a large mixing bowl. Let them mash it, knead it, and beat it. The longer and harder it is mixed, beaten, and pounded, the better it is. Roll into balls. Bake on cookie sheet at 350° for ten to twelve minutes. *Yield: 36.*

ME CRACKERS

You'll Need: enough round crackers so that each child can have two, slices of cheese or a cheese spread, olives sliced in half, pimentos, and raisins.

Here's How: Have children place cheese or spread on the crackers. Using the olives, pimentos, and raisins as facial features, have the children create two different expressions on the cracker face. Have them take turns telling about their faces, explaining when and why they felt that way. After discussion, allow faces to be eaten.

ME FACES

You'll Need: sliced bread, a small can of chopped olives or raisins, an eight-ounce jar of cheese spread or whipped cream cheese, shredded wheat biscuits or shredded coconut, sliced cherries, and pretzel sticks.

Here's How: Have children remove the crust from the bread. Then spread cheese over the entire area. Have the children create a face on the bread. Use cherries and olives for eyes and mouth. Use the pretzel sticks for nose. Use the coconut or shredded wheat as hair. Allow for a sharing time for the children to present their creations to the class before eating them.

COOKIE FRIENDS

You'll Need: two tablespoons of butter or margarine, two tablespoons of sugar, one tablespoon of egg (beat an egg and measure out one tablespoon), one quarter cup plus two tablespoons of flour, shredded coconut, raisins, and small gingerbread men cookie cutters.

Here's How: Mix butter and sugar with a wooden spoon. Push butter and sugar against the side of the bowl until well mixed. Slowly add egg to the mixture and beat well. Sift flour into mixture and fold in. Roll out dough on floured board to about one quarter inch. Have children cut out people shapes in the dough. Decorate the faces with raisins and coconut. Place on cookie sheet and bake for ten minutes at 350° degrees. Cookies should be light brown. *Yield: 24.*

GINGERBREAD PEOPLE

You'll Need: one cup of butter, one cup of sugar, one cup of dark molasses, one egg, two tablespoons vinegar, five cups sifted flour, one and one half teaspoons salt, two teaspoons ginger, one teaspoon cinnamon, one teaspoon cloves, sprinkles, raisins, and nuts

Here's How: Cream butter and add sugar gradually. Beat in egg, molasses, and vinegar. Blend in sifted dry ingredients. Chill, and then roll out to one eighth to one quarter inch thick on lightly floured surface. Cut into shapes with cookie cutter. Place on lightly greased cookie sheet. Have children decorate the cookies. Children may want happy or sad faces depending on how they are feeling. After decoration, bake at 375° for five to fifteen minutes depending on the size and thickness of the cookies.

MY DESSERT

You'll Need: three-ounce package of strawberry-flavored gelatin, one cup of boiling water, three quarters of a cup cold water, and an eight-ounce container of strawberry yogurt

Here's How: Dissolve the gelatin in the boiling water and then add the cold water until slightly thickened. Next add the yogurt. Use an electric beater to beat until mixture is very fluffy and light. Have the children pour the fluffy mixture into individual dishes or cups. Let the dessert chill for about two hours so that it is firm. Use the cereal that is in the shape of the letters of the alphabet and have the children put their name or nickname on the dessert as a topping.

LET'S FACE IT

You'll Need: one package of instant pudding and pie filling, two cups of milk, gumdrops, jelly beans, raisins, coconut, miniature marshmallows, and chocolate chips

Here's How: Follow the directions for making the pudding as printed on the package. Allow the mixture to stand to set for about five minutes. Have the children spoon out dessert into paper cups. Allow the children to decorate the top of the dessert as a face. Use the ingredients listed above as eyes, nose, mouth, hair, and so on. Provide for a sharing time for the children to present their creations to the class, explaining their choices of expression and ingredients.

7

Activities in
the Language Arts

The language arts activities included in this chapter help the teacher to enhance the child's self-image through reading, poetry, and creative writing experiences. Language arts is an integral part of every learning experience for the young child, and if these activities are presented in a non-threatening and supportive manner the child will readily respond to you and them. A child's thoughts and ideas should be accepted and not criticized.

Children should be able to discover how they perceive themselves and the relationships they have with others through the use of these activities. By exploring their feelings and thoughts, children are able to get a feeling of "self."

The activities presented may be done by the whole class, small groups, or individually at learning centers. You may adapt them to meet the needs of your class and present the materials in the manner in which you feel most comfortable. Individuality adds spice to the activities and the classroom.

Children will become more aware of themselves while using these activities and taking part in the discussions that are sure to follow if the atmosphere in your room is conducive to developing a positive self-concept. None of the activities presented will be of value if you do not encourage the children to feel good about themselves and their accomplishments.

Young children may use many of the writing activities by using a tape recorder, or dictating a story to you, or by drawing pictures on which you can write their thoughts and ideas.

As with all the activities presented in the book, their success or failure depends for a large part on you, the teacher. If the children in your class feel comfortable, secure, and good about themselves, these activities should provide you both with stimulating and enjoyable experiences.

IT'S ME

To discover how children view themselves and what things they would like to change.

You'll Need: paper large enough to trace each child's hand, scissors, pencils

Here's How: Have each child trace his hand on paper and cut it out. On one side the child writes down three words to describe himself. On the other side he writes three words that he wished described himself. Children meet in small groups to discuss responses and ways of changing or improving.

ANONYMOUS WRITING

Children write suggestions, complaints, or ideas about school, family, etc.

You'll Need: a cardboard box to serve as a class mailbox, paper, pencils

Here's How: Allow the children to write about their feelings, complaints, ideas, suggestions, likes, dislikes, etc. without recording their names. Have some read aloud to class and discuss responses and reactions.

BEING REPORTERS

First day of school activity to help children get to know each other.

You'll Need: pencils, paper

Here's How: Divide the class into pairs; if an odd number, the teacher joins the activity. Allow five minutes for the students to find out as much as possible about one another. Suggested areas are birthdays, family, pets, summer vacation, favorite things, hobbies, etc. At the end of the time limit, meet in a circle. Have each child introduce his partner and tell what he learned from the interview.

ONE SPECIAL THING

To help students appreciate and respond to one another.

Here's How: Divide the class into pairs; if an odd number, the teacher joins in. Allow five minutes for the children to converse freely. At the time limit, meet in a circle to discuss responses. Each person should tell a special thing about his partner that makes him special or important to the group.

QUESTIONNAIRE

First day of school activity to get to know each other.

You'll Need: a questionnaire listing such items as—Who's tallest? Who's oldest? Who's wearing the widest belt? Who's missing teeth? Who has the longest hair?

Here's How: Distribute a copy of the questionnaire to each student. Allow them to move freely around the room to talk to each other to find out which children fit the descriptions. After a time limit, meet in a circle to discuss responses and children's reactions to the activity.

SPECIAL DAY

Assign each child a special day of the month. On that day trace around the child's body. Ask him to bring a baby picture to class. Discuss the changes that have taken place—how has he grown? What new things can he do? Decorate and paint the body tracing and display it with the baby picture.

RAINY DAY FEELINGS

Help young children explore their feelings on a rainy day when they must stay indoors. Put two umbrellas in the quiet corner so that children can sit under them to read or talk. Ask them to name the good things about rainy days. Discuss their feelings. Add some music to the umbrella corner—"Raindrops Keep Fallin' on My Head" or "Rainy Days and Mondays."

DEAR KIDS

A letter from the class to themselves can stimulate language development and clarify thoughts and feelings that they have about themselves and school.

You'll Need: language experience chart paper, crayons, envelopes, stamps

Here's How: Ask each child to contribute something he likes to do in school and something he likes about himself. Pictures may be added to the letters. Encourage children to talk about themselves and their families. When letters to the class are complete, a trip to the post office or mailbox can conclude the lesson. When letters arrive, read aloud to entire class and discuss.

ALL ABOUT ME BOOKLETS

A collection of stories, poems, and artwork created by the student that expresses ideas about himself.

You'll Need: large construction paper for the cover of the booklets, paper, art materials, pencils

Here's How: The cover of each booklet should be a self-portrait of the student. Booklet should contain papers written by the student expressing his feelings, goals, hopes, ideas, etc. Collection and addition of material should continue throughout the year.

THE GREAT ME

This is a collection of information about each child created by the teacher. The teacher conducts individual interviews, taking notes on family, hobbies, goals, likes, etc. Teacher types out the information on each child and staples it together in a booklet. Each child designs a cover and illustrates pages of the book. Title each book *The Great Me* with the child's name. These books should be available in the classroom all year long so that the children can learn about their classmates.

I LIKE YOU

Each child receives a booklet written by others in the class telling why he is liked or admired by them.

You'll Need: one picture of each child, paper, pencils

Here's How: Each day choose one child. On that day, the other children write down the things they like about the chosen child. Collect the papers and form a booklet. Put the child's picture on the cover and present it to him.

STORY STARTERS

To offer an opportunity to the student to practice writing skills while expressing important facts and information about himself.

You'll Need: index cards, paper, pencils

Here's How: Put "Story Starters" on cards and allow students to select the ones they wish to write about. Suggestions:

1. If I had ten wishes . . .
2. If I were the teacher, I would . . .
3. If I were a parent, I would . . .
4. Things I really like about myself are . . .
5. The happiest day of my life was when . . .

WANTED POSTERS

Each child creates a poster about himself expressing important information.

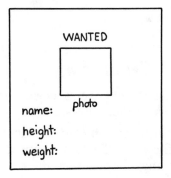

You'll Need: pictures of each child, drawing paper, pencils, ink pad

Here's How: Have each child complete a "Wanted Poster" of himself. Paste the child's picture on the top of the poster. Leave a space to put the fingerprints. Have the child fill in the following information on his poster.

Name	Weight	Special Remarks
Nicknames	Height	Friends
Address	Hair	Favorites
Birthday	Eyes	
Place of Birth	Interests	
Age	Hobbies	

LET'S LEARN ABOUT ME

This activity helps children describe themselves in positive ways.

You'll Need: construction paper, crayons, markers

Here's How: The children print their names in large letters on the paper. The letters should be in a vertical position. Have them find words to describe themselves that begin with the letters of their name. Example:

M — many friends
A — active
R — ready to work
Y — young

GUESS WHO

A game that challenges children's powers of observation and experience in expressing themselves.

Here's How: The teacher or a child gives clues to the identity of one of the children in the class. The clues can be physical (clothing, height, etc.) or they may describe the interests or abilities of the child. Example: This child loves to draw and sing. Today this child is wearing sneakers. Who is it?

WHAT BUGS YOU

Children have the chance to explore their feelings and to express their complaints or pet peeves.

You'll Need: construction paper, pipe cleaners, crayons, scissors, glue

Here's How: Have the children cut out colored circles. Glue the edges of the circles together to form the body of a caterpillar. Use the pipe cleaners as feelers. On each circle have the child write down something that "bugs" him. Display the bugs on a special bulletin board or on their desks.

WHEN ANGER STRIKES

To help children cope with anger by thinking and writing about the things that make them angry.

You'll Need: paper, pencils, crayons

Here's How: Have each child write down ten things that make him angry. Then ask each child to read over the list and try to explain why each one causes anger. Have the children write down an explanation of each situation and why it makes them angry. Draw pictures to go with the sentences to explain their feelings.

IF I WERE

Creative writing exercise to express feelings and emotions.

You'll Need: pencils, paper

Here's How: Have each child write a story about what it would be like to be something else. Give suggestions like being an animal, the pencil sharpener, a television, a musical instrument, etc. Have the child explain his choice of object and what it would feel like to be it. As a follow-up activity, have the child draw himself as that object.

I'M GLAD I'M ME

To enhance the child's feeling of self-worth.

You'll Need: pencil, paper, drawing paper, crayons

Here's How: Have each child write a story with the title "I'm Glad I'm Me." Have them explain in the story the reasons that they are glad to be themselves. Add pictures of the children and their family or friends.

WE AND ME

The children become aware of physical likenesses in one another.

You'll Need: a full-length mirror, a cassette tape recorder

Here's How: Two or three children sit on the floor before a mirror. The rest of the group sits or stands behind them. All of the children look in the mirror and tell what makes them look alike. Take turns getting in front of the mirror. Place the recorder with the children. Assign each one a partner. The partners take turns in front of the mirror, noting what makes them look alike. They discuss their likenesses on tape. Later they can observe their differences.

MAGIC CARPETS

Take a magic carpet ride and talk about the things you see.

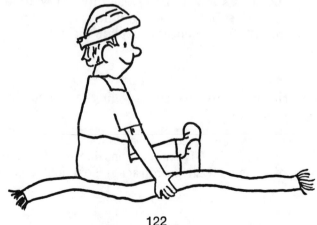

You'll Need: carpet squares, Rimsky-Korsakoff's "Scheherazade," record player.

Here's How: Put the record on the record player, and ask the children to sit on their magic carpets. Encourage each child to tell something that he "sees" from his carpet. When children are comfortable with expressing themselves, they tend to have good feelings about themselves. Use the carpet approach to sight situations that may have been problems in the classroom. Example: "I see two boys fighting over a ball. Do you see that? I wonder what should be done."

WHEN I GROW UP

A discussion of various careers and what children want to be. This kind of discussion helps build self-images and gives an additional opportunity to use language.

You'll Need: magazines, newspapers, construction paper, scissors, glue

Here's How: Ask the children to look through the magazines to find pictures to represent his or her job. For preschoolers, a small group may look through the magazine with the teacher and select the pictures that the children show an interest in. The pictures can be cut and pasted on construction paper. The teacher asks for comments from each child. The children can write their comments or dictate them to the teacher, depending on their age level. The stories and pictures can then be arranged on a bulletin board.

HEADLINE COLLAGE

Children use cut-out newspaper words to tell about themselves.

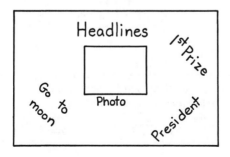

You'll Need: newspapers, scissors, glue, construction paper, child's snapshot or self-portrait

Here's How: Give the children newspapers and ask them to look for headline words that describe them or tell their ambitions (good, handsome, best, etc.). Place a snapshot in the center of a large piece of construction paper. Glue the words the child has selected around his picture.

Follow-up: Ask the children to explain their choice of words.

POETRY

ME

My smile belongs to a special face,
My nose has found a perfect place.
And my eyes, they're just right for me,
And this mouth, well, you can see,
The parts all fit together, to make the
Puzzle that is ME!

ME IS A GOOD THING TO BE

Although you say I'm only three,
I know ME *is a good thing to be!*
There's so many more things that I can do,
That I couldn't do when I was two.
And I'm sure that I'll do much more,
When I get as old as four!
The whole wide world's out there for me,
And I know that "Me's a good thing to be!"

THE MIRROR

When you look in the mirror, what do you see?
Is it the someone that you want to be?
Does the someone like blue, or best of all, red?
Does the someone choose chocolate, or vanilla instead?
Does the someone like puddles for splashing about?
Or is the someone wishing for the sun to come out?
When you look in the mirror, do you like what you see?
Are you happy to say, "I like being me?"

THE AUTUMN CHILDREN

Playing, Saying
Seeing, Being
Needing, Leading
Crying, Sighing
Living, Giving
Shoving, Loving
Yearning, Learning
Growing, Knowing
Too Soon Going

I'LL BE THE SUN

You want so much for me to shine
In the light you've made for me,
But I think that you should know,
That that can never be.

Unlike the moon, I am the sun.
I'll make my own spotlight.
Don't worry Mom; don't worry Dad;
Somehow I'll turn out right.

I have to grow up my way,
To think, to do, and be,
The very special person
I've come to know as me!

YOU LIGHT UP MY LIFE

From Mrs. Graham to her preschoolers

I like the way you've learned to learn.
I like the way you wait your turn.

I like the way you've begun to share.
I like the way you've grown to care.

You light up my life.

I like the way you make your plan,
And that you say, "I know I can!"

I like the way you sing and play.
And that you know you're Special, today and every day.

You light up my life.

I like the way you color and have
learned to print your name.
In many ways, you're different, and
yet you're still the same.

You light up my life.

Little children who have come so far
And still have far to go,

Can you see what you've done for me?
Yes, I think you know.

You light up my life.

GERMAINE'S MEAN GREEN MACHINE

Mother watches Germaine go past,
A worried look on her face.
But he knows the green machine
is going to win the race.

When Germaine rides his green machine
he feels just like a king,
He's the best at what he does,
the best at everything.

It's not the speed that makes it great,
It's just the feelin' free.
When Germaine's on the green machine
it's the only place to be.

Everyone needs something to make him
outshine the sun,
Germaine found his green machine
makes him number one!

HAPPY

Tanida's smart, she's on the ball.
She surely will succeed.

But Tanida said, "I just want to be happy,
that's really all I need."

And so her teacher deeply thought of the
words of this little one.

When we begin their learning, do we forget
their fun?

*Children laugh and learn at play and need
    lots of time to grow.*

*They're only ours for a little while,
And too soon they go.*

*If they find happiness in learning, in
    their own time and place,*

*Could these leaders of tomorrow,
    make our world a better place?*

ALONE

*I had to sit alone today,
For making too much noise, they say.*

*I guess I'll never learn, when to talk,
When to listen and how to wait my turn.*

*It's just that there's so many words
Inside of me to say,
I want to share my thoughts with you,
And waiting gets in the way.*

*But tomorrow will be better,
I'll sit up straight and tall.*

*And you'll know I've learned my lesson,
When I don't talk at all!*

POETRY FROM THE PRESCHOOL ROOM

PAINTING AT THE EASEL

Red, blue, green, yellow
Pretty paint in glass jars.

Long fuzzy brushes
Dipping, dripping.

Clean, white paper waiting
Making strokes, up and down, over and over.

Wide lines, thin lines, houses, faces, me.

Mixing colors
catching drips.

Today I'll paint a feeling
Cover my paper with RED paint.

How do I feel?

ART AREA

Scissors, colored paper, and bottles
*   filled with glue,*
I love to go to the art area, there's
*   so much there to do.*

I paste and cut and color, until it's
*   clean up time,*
Then I take my picture to Daddy,
He loves it cause it's Mine.

He hangs it on the 'frigerator for everyone to
*   see,*
And that makes me feel special, cause I know
*   he's*

Proud of me!

QUIET AREA

I have a favorite puzzle, that I do each day,
I do it once, I do it twice, before it's
*   put away.*

Beads, buttons, books on shelves,
Waiting here for me.

So many things to touch and do,
It's my favorite place to be!

UP IN THE LOFT

We have a loft in our room,
It's blue and yellow and high.

It has a ladder and we play fireman there
*   and read sometimes.*

It's a good place to go when no one
*   wants to play with you.*

It's my hiding place,
Sometimes kids need to hide,
I do.

BLOCK AREA

All shapes and sizes of blocks.

You build all day, a city or a town.

*Then somebody comes and knocks your block
town down!*

HOUSEKEEPING

*"You be the Mommy. I'll be the Daddy.
You make dinner for Me."*

*That's what we do in housekeeping,
pretending what we'll be.*

*But things have changed along the way,
Now just take a look.*

Mommy is a doctor and Daddy is the cook!

MUSIC AREA

*My teacher lets me put the needle on the
record all by myself.*

*If it makes a loud, scratchy sound.
She doesn't care.
She wants me to feel big.*

A SONG ABOUT COLORS*

I like red, *the color makes me merry! It's the color of an apple and the color of a cherry.*

I like orange. *It's the best of all. It's the color of a pumpkin and pretty leaves in the fall!*

I like yellow, it's the special one! It's the color of bananas and the color of the sun!

I like green, *it feels so good to me. It's the color of grass and the color of the sea.*

I like white. *I think you would like to know. It's the color of my bread and the color of the snow!*

I like brown. *It's the color for me. It's the color of cookies and the color of coffee.*

I like blue, *let me tell you why. It's the color of my crayon and the color of the sky!*

I like black, *the color is just dandy! It's the color of the darkness and the color of licorice candy!*

To sing or play: GG/ECC/DCBA/GGG/GGFE/DBGG/GGAB/C

OUR AIDE

by Terry Graham and her 36 preschool children

Our aide is a teacher, a helper, a guide.
She makes us feel happy when we hurt down inside.
She takes care of money for lunches and trips.
She always knows stories of pirates and ships.
She's never too busy to take time to play,
Or listen to anything we have to say.
She answers our questions and pretty poems tells.
She never talks mean to us, gets angry or yells.
Our aide makes us aware of plants, flowers, and spring.
She likes to play games with us and to teach us to sing.
She helps us to paint, and she's a good cleaner-upper.
And when she comes in Housekeeping, we cook her supper.
When we say "we can't," she helps us to try.
She takes care of us, if we get sick or cry.
Our aide says we're "special," she wants us to know.
And we think she's special, so we'll just tell her so.

YOU ARE SPECIAL

8

Science, Mathematics, and Self-Discovery

Young children have a need to know about themselves. They enjoy discovering and learning for themselves. The experiences in this chapter give children opportunities to explore their feelings, learn about their bodies, and understand their uniqueness, as well as develop math skills through self-discovery and self-exploration.

When using these activities, let interests, reactions, and questions come from the children themselves. Recognizing the children's contributions as worthwhile and important, helps them to realize their own importance. The child who receives this type of response from adults will be more confident and eager to participate in future situations. Participation will grow in quality as well as quantity.

It is generally agreed that physical self-concept develops before psychological self-concept. One result of this is the continuing influence of the physical on the psychological. In order to develop the most positive feelings about the self, children should understand and appreciate the "specialness" of their bodies. Experiences in measurement and comparing differences, and graphing add to the child's concept of body awareness. Feeling good about one's body generates good feelings about the "total self."

Children need to cope with their emotions, anxieties, and fears. Letting children know that anger and fear are emotions we all experience and are acceptable ways to feel, helps children realize that they are worthwhile individuals when they display these emotions.

The importance of the dynamic relationship between the physical and the psychological self-concepts would be difficult to overstate. We should take every opportunity to help children explore each of these areas in a positive, non-threatening way.

MATHEMATICS

GRAPH IT (3rd and up)

To encourage students to become more aware of the likenesses and differences of their peers.

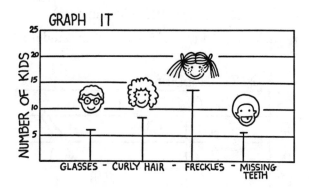

You'll Need: graph paper, colored pencils
Here's How: Have each student make a bar graph to show various characteristics of classmates. Suggestions: freckles, curly hair, glasses, lost teeth, etc. Children then circulate around the room to find children with those traits and they record them on the graph. Display the results in a math center or bulletin board.

FAMILY FACTS (3rd and up)

To create an interest and awareness of family structure, both similarities and differences.

You'll Need: paper, pencils
Here's How: Have the children record answers to these questions about their families:

1. What is the sum of all the ages of the family members?
2. What is the difference between the ages of the oldest and youngest?
3. What is the sum of the ages of the female members; males?
4. What is the sum of those members older than yourself?
5. What is the sum of those younger?
6. What is the difference between the number of adults and children? Male to female?

Provide a sharing time to compare and discuss answers.

GRAPH HOBBIES (3rd and up)

To explore various activities and hobbies of the students within the class.

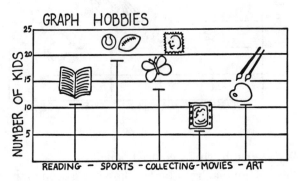

You'll Need: paper, colored pencils

Here's How: Have the students gather information from one another concerning leisure activities. Students should prepare a graph to illustrate the information. Plan a sharing time to discover which activities are most popular or unique.

THREE WISHES (3rd and up)

To provide an opportunity for children to express wishes for objects and to make comparisons.

You'll Need: paper, pencils, catalogs

Here's How: Gather the class together in a circle for an explanation of the activity. Each child is allowed $100.00 to spend on any three items found in the catalog. Children work individually or in small groups. Each records the price of the item and subtracts it from the $100.00. They proceed until three objects are bought and the total is not more than $100.00. Return to the circle to share purchases.

TELLING TIME (1st—3rd grade)

Help the children learn about time by using their bodies to create a clock.

You'll Need: a circle on the floor made with a rug or tablecloth, paper numbers from one to twelve

Here's How: Ask twelve children to place themselves on the circle clock. Choose two children to be the hands of the clock. The children who are the hands lie on the floor in the center telling the time you specify. Give turns to everyone who wishes to be the hands of the clock.

KID COMPUTATIONS (3rd and up)

A challenge of math skills can also get children to discover each other. Begin by forming the class into small groups.

Here's How: Put these questions on the board or on ditto sheets. Make problems to fit your individual students.

1. Total number of blue-eyed children?
2. Total ages?
3. Number of birthdays in December?
4. The total number of pets? dogs? fish?
5. How many students' favorite color is red?
6. Total number of students whose favorite flavor of ice cream is chocolate?
7. Add your house or apartment number to 13.
8. Add the year you were born to the current year.
9. How many children are Libras? Aquarians?
10. Total toes? Fingers?

FEELING GRAPH (3rd and up)

Help the children explore feelings and enhance graphing skills.

FEELING GRAPH

	1	2	3	4	5	6	7	8	9
ANGRY	■	■							
LONELY	■	■	■	■					
EXCITED									
BORED									

You'll Need: paper, pencils

Here's How: Ask the children to list, on lined paper, several feelings they think they will experience during the week. Each time they express that feeling, they put a check next to it on their chart. At the end of the week, ask the class to make a bar graph representing the number of times they felt and expressed their feelings. When the graphs are complete, compare and discuss them.

SCIENCE AND SELF-DISCOVERY

SHOOT FOR THE STARS (Pre-K and up)

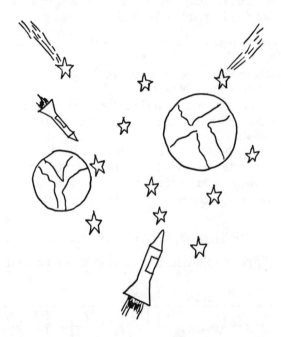

To encourage improvement of personal skills while learning about the solar system.

You'll Need: bulletin board, star cut-outs, moons, planets, rocket ships, markers, crayons, pins

Here's How: Display on your bulletin board the sun and the planets with their moons. Line up rocket ship cut-outs along the bottom of the board. As a child makes a positive effort and shows improvement in an area, he selects a rocket ship, signs his name and pins it to a planet, moon or star, in space. Rocket ships are used to reward good workers.

Examples: improved printing, punctuality, memorizing multiplication facts, completing homework, extra credit work, etc.

Variation: hold a contest for one week—winners are those who have earned the most rockets in space

JOBS (Pre-K and up)

To encourage students to make generalizations and categorize choices of career interests.

You'll Need: paper, pencils, scissors, magazines

Here's How: Students cut out pictures of people at work doing jobs that they may be interested in doing someday. Place the pictures on a board and number each one. The teacher makes statements about the careers and the children record which picture fits the statement. Provide time to discuss answers and career selections. Sample statements:

Which jobs are usually outdoors?
Which jobs are done alone?
What careers deal with children?
Which jobs need special training or education?
Which jobs seem to be more fun than work?
Which jobs seem dangerous?
What careers seem to help others?

CLOUD FORMATIONS

Read *It Looked Like Spilt Milk* by Charles G. Shaw.

You'll Need: A day when the sky is blue, with big puffy, white clouds, paper, pencils (optional)

Here's How: Take your class outdoors. Sit on the ground and watch the clouds. Ask the children to look at the clouds and imagine them to be something. They will soon be describing animals, cars, or people. Have the class tell or write about their experiences. Did everyone see the same formations and imagine them to be the same things? Talk about individual interpretations.

THE FIVE SENSES

The following activities are concerned with the five senses. They help children develop positive self-concepts through body awareness. Preschool children and older will benefit from the experiences when the teacher varies the level to make it appropriate for each age group.

INTRODUCTION

Read: *My Five Senses* by Aliki.

Create a "Five Senses" Book. Here are some suggestions.

Page 1. Ditto these words for young children, "I Can See, I See With My Eyes"

> *Examples:* *Child draws a self-portrait*
> *Child may choose a picture from a magazine of something he sees on the way to school*
> *Give each child a small square of tin foil to be a mirror: I See Me!*

Page 2. "I Can Hear, I Hear With My Ears"

Ditto a guitar; help the children staple a rubber band to it and they can pluck or strum their guitars to make sounds.

Draw a picture of something you hear in the classroom, at home, or outside.

Page 3. "I Can Smell. I Smell With My Nose"

Give the children cloves, mint, and coffee to glue to their papers

Put perfume on a cotton ball and glue it on the paper.

Page 4. "I Can Touch. I Touch With My Fingers"
Let the children choose different textures to glue on this page (sandpaper, cotton, wood, foil).

Page 5. "I Can Taste. I Taste With My Tongue"
Give each child two pieces of candy or gum, one to glue, and one to eat.

WHAT DO I SEE? (Pre-K and up)

Place this guessing game in your science center.

You'll Need: Baby food jars, bottles, or clear containers

Here's How: Put samples of the following in containers. Encourage the children to identify the contents by using their sense of sight: flour, sugar, tea, coffee, grass seed, corn, rice, macaroni, baking soda, cornstarch, cereal, sesame seeds.

Older children enjoy describing the attributes of all the white substances. Younger children need supervision and more common materials should be used.

MORE SIGHT EXPLORATION ACTIVITIES

FIVE SENSES (sight)

You'll Need: milk cartons, liquid detergent, food coloring, straws

Here's How:

1. Fill milk cartons with half parts water and detergent. Give the children straws. Ask them what color bubbles they would like and let them add food coloring to the mixture. Watch their surprise as they blow colored bubbles.
2. Use food coloring and muffin tins to mix and create new colors.

3. Give the children one sheet of paper to hold behind them. Encourage them to tear a shape: square, circle, triangle. Younger children can tear the shapes and glue them to another sheet of paper. What does your torn picture look like?

4. Look at two objects. How are they alike? How are they different? How many words can you think of to describe them?

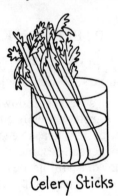

Celery Sticks

5. Place a stalk of celery in a glass of water with red food coloring added to it. Ask the class to observe what happens. Try the same experiment with white carnations. They will turn red, too!

6. Obtain a large carton that a small child will be able to get into. Ask the class to close their eyes as you select one child to get into the box. As you or a child describe the child in the box, others guess.

WHAT DO I HEAR? (Pre-K and up)

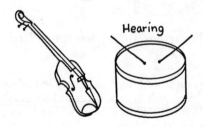

Hearing

You'll Need: tape recorder

Here's How: Tape sounds heard in the home or at school. Ask the children to identify them as you play them one at a time. Here are some sound ideas:

typewriter	alarm clock
school bell	water running
door slamming	animal sounds

Follow-up: Read *An Ear is to Hear* by Jan Slepian and Ann Seidler.

MORE SOUND EXPLORATION ACTIVITIES

1. "What Did I Do?"

   Blindfold one child in the center of the circle. Ask another child to perform an action that makes a sound: clap, slide, run. The child guesses the sound he hears.

2. "Croc and Captain Hook"

   One child hides as the crocodile with a loud ticking alarm clock. Another child as Captain Hook tries to find the croc by listening for the clock.

3. "Listen, Sh! Sh!"

   The children close their eyes and take turns telling the classroom sounds that they hear.

4. "Discrimination"

   Put objects on the table whose sounds are very different: keys, wooden blocks, fork. While the children have their eyes closed, drop one object on the floor. Ask them to identify that object. Challenge the children to tell how the sounds are different.

5. "Sound Tricks"

   Place four objects in a row on the table. Ask the children to look at each object as you name it. Make an error and see if the children are listening.

6. "Mother Cat and Her Kittens"

   The children find hiding places in the room. They are lost kittens. One child acts as Mother searching for her babies as they meow for her. When Mother Cat finds one kitten, together they hunt for the rest.

7. **"Animal Sounds"**

   Make different animal sounds and ask the children to tell the animal that makes that sound. Allow the children to make the sounds too!

8. **"Picture the Sound"**

   Make a variety of sounds for the children. If you could see that sound, what would it look like? Ask them to color, paint, or fingerpaint their impressions of the sound.

9. **"Echo Claps"**

   Ask the children to listen as you clap or beat a rhythm. See if they can echo your sound.

10. **"Listen and Count"**

    Have one child stand with his back to you. Play three beats on a triangle. See if the child can count the beats in his head. Play loud and soft sounds. Can your students discriminate?

11. **"Vibrations 1"**

    In your construction area, help the children hammer nails on wood scraps. Stretch rubber bands across the nails to make a guitar. Strum the "strings" and watch the vibrations that create sound.

12. **"Vibrations 2"**

    Strike a tuning fork and place it in a pan of water. Ask the children to observe.

13. **"Listen and Move"**

    Obtain a metronome. Ask the class to listen and move to fast/slow rhythms.

14. **"Tap and Listen"**

    Give the children rhythm sticks and have them tap different objects in the room: wall, chair, door, floor. What sounds do you hear?

SPOON SOUNDS

You'll Need: plastic tops, bowls, pieces of wood, pan, styrofoam block, paper, wooden spoon

Here's How: A child selects three objects. Show him the wooden spoon and ask, "If you hit the objects with a spoon, which will make the loudest sound? the softest? the same sound?"

SOFT/LOUD GAME

You'll Need: containers for shaking, fillers (sand, coins, rice, beans, cotton, peas, feathers)

Here's How: Fill the containers with different amounts of fillers. Ask the children to listen as someone shakes the container. Which has the loudest sound? softest? What do you think is inside the container?

WHAT DO I FEEL?

1. "Things I Like to Touch"

THE FIVE SENSES

Things I like to touch

Velvet Fur
Carpet
Cotton
Soap
flakes

You'll Need: crayons, glue, a variety of textures

Here's How: Draw around each child's hand. At the end of his fingertips, have him glue objects he likes to touch.

2. "What Do You Feel?"

   Place pans of water of varied temperatures on a table. Ask the class to describe the differences.

3. "It's in the Bag"

You'll Need: a paper bag, objects to touch

Here's How: Place items in bag. Child reaches inside and holds one object. He must describe it and name it before taking it out.

Variations: Inside the bag place a bowl, a spoon, a wash cloth, a comb. Ask the child to find something you need to take a bath; something to put cereal in; something to make your hair look nice, etc.

To create another "Touch Box": Take the top off an oatmeal box. Cut the foot from an old sock and stretch it over the oatmeal box. The chidren put their hands through the sock and describe what you've hidden inside.

4. "Who Am I?"

Blindfold one child. Select another child for the blindfolded child to identify by using his sense of touch. Give hints if necessary.

5. "What Can it Be? Feel and See!"

Place a large object inside a pillow case. Encourage the class to describe the object. Can they guess what it might be? Record their observations and descriptions. Take the object out of the case and see what new words they come up with. Record those and compare.

SMELLING ACTIVITIES

1. "Spice is Nice"

You'll Need: square fabric scraps or tissue paper, things to smell

Here's How: Place about a teaspoon of cinnamon, coffee, chocolate, peppermint, and orange rind on the fabric or tissue paper. Lift the corners to make little bundles. Tie the top to secure. The children sniff each package and try to identify the scents.

2. "Nose Knows"

Use baby food jars with holes punched in the tops to hold good things to smell. Older children will enjoy the challenge of taped jars so that they cannot see the contents.

Variation: Cut holes in the top of a shoebox. Place oranges, cinnamon, or peppermint inside for identification.

3. "Recording Smells"

Sit outside and record the things you smell. Sit inside and repeat the activity. Compare the findings.

4. "Favorite Smells"

Ask the class to think about their favorite things to smell. Record. Use their thoughts to simulate some poetry.

WHAT DO I TASTE?

1. Place a common food in a bag (apple, cracker). Describe it for the children. When they guess it, have enough for everyone to taste. Encourage them to give their own descriptions. Make a language experience chart.

2. Ask a child to close his eyes and taste a food like cinnamon candies, sourballs, or fruit. Ask him to name the food and whether it was sweet or sour.

3. Breakfast—Ask your students to bring bread, oranges, and eggs to class. Divide the children into small groups, each in charge of preparing part of the meal.

   fresh-squeezed orange juice
   cinnamon toast
   scrambled eggs
   milk

   You may wish to provide breakfast foods not normally eaten by most children: grits, scrapple, biscuits, and a variety of jellies or preserves.

4. Give each child a soda cracker. Ask the children to hold their noses. Does the cracker taste the same? Try other varieties of crackers: Ritz, graham.

5. Have a mirror available so that the children can look at their taste buds. How do they feel? Identify which taste buds recognize sweet, sour, salty, bitter.

6. Use a medicine dropper to put different substances on the children's tongues. Where did you taste sugar? salt? peppermint? There are specific areas of the tongue for each taste.

149

FIVE SENSES REVIEW ACTIVITY

Have the children draw their self-portrait on a large sheet of construction paper. Divide the area around the picture into five parts. The areas are called sight, hearing, sound, touch, scent. Paste appropriate pictures in the five areas. Older children can write in words that describe things they see, feel, hear, and touch.

RESOURCES FOR THE FIVE SENSES

1. Filmstrips and Cassettes

   My Senses and Me Series, Encyclopedia Britannica, Educational Corp., 1971.

   Includes: "What Do I See When I Look?"
   "What Do I Hear When I Listen?"
   "What Do I Feel When I Touch?"
   "What Do I Smell When I Taste?"

2. Filmstrip and Record

   "My Five Senses," Soundstrip Film Library, Thomas Crowell and Co., N.Y., 1969.

LEARNING ABOUT OURSELVES

1. "Our Bodies" (3rd and up)

You'll Need: heavy brown wrapping paper, pencils, crayons, science books that show body parts

Here's How: Have the chldren form pairs. One student lies on the paper as the other traces an outline of his body. Using the science book, the children fill in the parts of the body (organs, bones, muscles).

2. "Head and Faces"

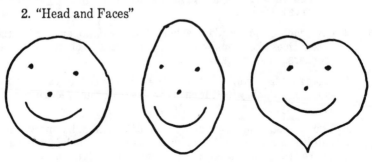

Talk about the shapes of faces. There are oval, oblong, heart-shaped, and round faces. What other shapes can you think of? What is the shape of your face?

Measure the children's heads in the same region. Measure the oldest and the youngest child. What do you notice? Then ask the children to bring in their baby pictures. Ask them what they observe about the size of a baby's head in relation to its body.

3. "Eyes"

　　a. Count the number of eyes of each color in the class and make a chart to indicate distribution.

BROWN	GREY	BLUE	GREEN	HAZEL

4. "Ears"

　　a. Look at the differences in ear lobes: free lobes and fixed. Ask the children to find out the kind of lobes their parents have.

　　b. Ring a bell and ask the children to tell the direction the sound came from.

　　c. *Echo*—Explore the sounds made in a room that has had all the furniture removed. Can a blindfolded child walk to a wall and get close without touching it by listening to his footsteps? Try it!

　　d. *Singing in a bucket*—What does it sound like? What is happening to the sound?

5. "Mouths"

　　a. Observe whether or not the children can roll their tongues. Who can fold his tongue? Folded and rolled tongues are hereditary traits. Ask the children to find out whether or not their parents can fold or roll their tongues.

　　b. Have the children look in the mirror. How do you look when you talk? Does your tongue move? Can some words be said without moving your tongue? Which ones?

6. "Feet"

　　a. *Touch Game*—Child removes his shoes. Hold an object against his foot. Ask him to identify it.

　　b. Can you tell boys' feet from girls' feet? Hide three children under a sheet with their feet sticking out. Whose feet are they? Class must guess.

151

7. "Arms and Hands"

 a. Measure each finger as you draw around the children's hands. How much can each of the children's hands pick up? Find out by putting some seeds in a can. Ask the children to pick up as many seeds as they can with their left hands, right hands. Transfer the seeds into another can and count them.

 b. Measure arms and forearms.

METRIC MEASURE

To gain practice in using metric measures and to encourage body awareness.

You'll Need: paper, pencils

Here's How: Have the students measure and record the following:

length of smallest finger
length of foot
length of strand of hair
distance from elbow to wrist
distance from knee to ankle
height standing, sitting

Compare and discuss answers. Who has the shortest hair? The longest foot? Who is the same height?

WHERE THERE'S A WILL, THERE'S A WEIGH
(Pre-K and up)

Introduce a center on weight and balance with the book *Weighing and Balancing*, by Jane Jonas Srivastava. Your center may include scales, mobiles, a balance beam, and objects to weigh. Write these questions on a chart and encourage the class to explore the center for the answers.

Does the tallest child weigh the most?
Do any two children weigh the same?
How much does our whole class weigh?

Beans, feathers, styrofoam, blocks, rice, and cotton make good weighing materials.

HAVE A HEART (3rd and up)

Try these questions on heartbeat.

Is your heartbeat faster or slower after exercise? Why?
Do you think your heartbeat speeds up or slows down when you're sleeping? Why?
How do you think your heart responds to surprise or to sudden noise?
Which picture is the true shape of your heart?

1.

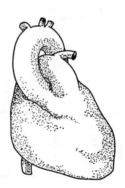

2.

Heartbeat Activities:

_____ Rest for five minutes
_____ Hop up and down twenty times
_____ Do jumping jacks for one minute
_____ Run in place for one minute
_____ Walk around the room three times

Heartbeat Rates After Activities

Activities																
Resting																
Hopping																
Jumping																
Singing																
Running																
Walking																

0 10 20 30 40 50 60 70 80 90 100 110 120 130 140 150

Heartbeat Per Minute

Name _____

THREE GUESSES (2nd and up)

To encourage observation and interest in the likenesses and differences in others.

You'll Need: paper, pencils

Here's How: Have the students sit in a circle so that everyone can see each other. Provide each child with a paper for an answer sheet and a pencil. The teacher makes a statement about one member of the group based on physical characteristics. Students record the name of the person who fits the description. Discuss the responses.

Examples: Who is taller than the persons on either side of the child described?

Who is sitting to the right of someone wearing glasses?

Who is closest to the smallest member of our class?

Who has the longest hair?

Who is closest to the clock?

PUTTING THE "ME" IN METRICS (2nd and up)

This activity develops metric measurement skills as well as body awareness.

You'll Need: large sheet of paper, metric tape measure, pencil/crayon, length of string, thumbtack, hook

Here's How: Give each child a line on the large sheet of paper, as in the illustration. Use the hook as a place to hang the tape measure. Fasten the string to the board with the thumbtack and tie the other end around the pencil or crayon. Each student finds his or her metric measurements and records the results.

SILHOUETTES (Pre-K and up)

Here's an old-fashioned idea that will make a special gift. Children will enjoy sitting for their portraits and learning about light and shadow.

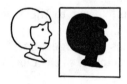

You'll Need: two sheets construction paper (contrasting colors), pencil, tape, light in the form of a lamp or flashlight

Here's How: Tape construction paper to the wall. Child sits in front of the paper. Use the bright light to cast a shadow of the child's profile on the paper. Teacher lightly traces the outlines with a pencil. Some children will be able to cut the silhouette out by themselves and glue it onto the contrasting background. Cover the silhouette with clear Contact paper or frame it.

ME IS A GOOD THING TO BE (Pre-K and up)

The children list their best characteristics and accomplishments on their self-portraits.

You'll Need: construction paper, crayons/markers

Here's How: Title each paper, "Me is a Good Thing to Be." Each child tells something he can do better than anyone else or his best characteristic. The child then draws his picture.

> *Example:* John: I read the most books
> Betty: I can climb the highest

Makes a great bulletin board!

WHO AM I? (Pre-K and up)

Children relate things that express who they are and what they feel. Introduce the activity by reading *Who Am I?* by J. Behrens.

You'll Need: construction-paper-made booklet with a page for each child

Here's How: Let each child answer the question "Who are You?" Record their answers and add to them throughout the year.

> *Example:* I am Mary. I like to have friends.

MY SYMBOL (Pre-K and up)

Here is a bulletin board that helps a child answer, "What is *Me*?"

You'll need: crayons/markers, board divided into squares, one for each member of your class

Here's How: Each student draws a symbol or picture of something that is meaningful to him—his likes, dislikes, loves, dreams, hopes.

PUZZLE DOLLS (Pre-K and up)

The children make a puzzle of themselves to aid in learning body parts.

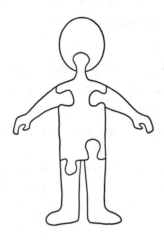

You'll Need: tagboard pattern of doll, crayons, pencils, pinking shears, construction paper

Here's How: The children trace the doll pattern onto their paper. They add their facial features and draw the clothing that matches what they are wearing that day.

Use the pinking shears to cut the doll into puzzle pieces. Before cutting, laminate or cover with clear Contact paper for a doll that will last.

MOVABLE DOLLS (Pre-K and 1st)

Children become acquainted with their own movable parts with this activity.

You'll Need: oaktag pre-cut ovals, circles or patterns that young children can trace, pencils/crayons, scissors, brass fasteners, hole punch

Here's How: Cut eight medium ovals, four small ovals, one large oval for the body, and one circle for the head. Punch holes where the pieces are to be joined together. The results will be a movable doll when you secure the joints with brass fasteners. Preschoolers may enjoy the dolls as puzzles if you use Velcro to fasten the joints together. The doll can then be taken apart and put together.

PAPER DOLL STICK PUPPETS

The children make puppets to look like themselves.

You'll Need: ditto or pattern of doll, wooden craft sticks, stapler, crayons or markers

Here's How: Have the children cut the ditto doll form or trace the pattern. Then add clothes and facial features. Staple the doll to a craft stick and put the child's name on the bottom.

FRAMED! (Pre-K and up)

The children frame pictures of themselves to be displayed in the classroom.

You'll Need: snapshots, styrofoam meat trays, glue, yarn/ribbon, hole punch, wallpaper

Here's How: Decorate the meat tray with a piece of wallpaper from a wallpaper book. The children glue their snapshots in the middle of the frame. Punch two holes at the top to thread the yarn or ribbon through. Tie in a bow and use as a hanger.

FAMILY BOARD (1st and up)

Children will become aware of family members and take pride in being an important part of their families.

You'll Need: your bulletin board covered with white paper, markers, family snapshots

Here's How: Write family words such as sister, brother, father, mother, along the edge of the board with markers, creating a border. Have the class bring in photographs of their families to display on the board. During your sharing time, discuss each photo.

PLAYDOUGH FAMILY

The children make families from playdough.

You'll Need: playdough, markers, tagboard, rubber cement

Here's How: Follow the playdough recipe on page 42. Have the children roll a ball of playdough for each member of their family. Add faces with markers. Write, "My Family" or "The Graham Family" on the tagboard and arrange the family members in order on it. Use the rubber cement to fix the playdough to the board. The dough will harden.

Variation: The children draw family trees on the tagboard. They then arrange their families on the appropriate branches of the tree.

FAMILY HISTORY (3rd and up)

The children interview parents and relatives about recent or long ago family stories. The class creates a "Family History Book" that is a collection of all the stories.

MY FAMILY AND ME (Pre-K and up)

You'll Need: a ditto that is headed "My Family and Me" and contains the questions below

Here's How: Have the children fill in the ways members are alike and the ways they are different by answering the following questions.

Everyone in my family likes to eat _____
Everyone in my family has _____
Everyone in my family likes to watch _____ on TV
Everyone in my family likes _____
No one likes _____

WHO IS IT? (Pre-K and Kindergarten)

Here is a game that helps children get to know each other and develop the concept of "what's missing?"

Everyone in the group closes his eyes and the teacher selects one child to leave the room. The teacher may or may not give clues to the identity of the missing child. The children try to guess who is missing.

NAME TRAINS (Pre-K to 1st)

The children take pride in themselves as they learn to recognize their names.

You'll Need: tagboard, markers

Here's How: Make tagboard train cars with the children's names on them. Put the cars on your bulletin board. Write the children's first names on cards that are the same length as the train cars. Encourage the children to match the cards to those on the train.

WHO'S THAT IN THE MIRROR? (Pre-K and Kindergarten)

You'll Need: a full-length mirror

Here's How: The children take turns looking at themselves in the mirror and following these directions:

smile	bend
turn around	say "Hello"
wave	say "Good-bye"

NAME DESIGNS (3rd and up)

Names are very important to children. This activity gives each child's name a unique importance.

You'll Need: plain paper, pencils, markers, or colored pencils

Here's How: Fold the paper in half. Ask the children to write their names in cursive so that the letters touch the folds of the paper. Tops or bottoms of letters can touch and fold. With a pencil, rub on the back of the written side, covering the entire area where the name is written. Open the paper and find your new name design.

Follow-up: Teach "My Name" by Jeffrey Moss in *The Sesame Street Song Book*, Children's Television Workshop, 1971.

A ROSE IS A ROSE (Pre-K and up)

Discuss the student's names. How many have middle names? Do the children know where their names came from and what they mean? What are the advantages of having three names? Do some children have more than three names?

Follow-up: Read *The Pocket Encyclopedia of Baby Names* (Globe Communications, 1978). Tell the children the meaning of their names.

HANDY HANDS (Pre-K and up)

Stimulate discussion about the wonder of hands.

You'll Need: mural paper, crayons/markers

Here's How: Trace around each child's hand on mural paper and ask him to color it. Encourage each child to tell you something his hands can do. If possible, invite older children to add their hands to your mural. What are the differences in the sizes of the hands of the older children? Adult handprints? Title your all-school mural, "Let's Join Hands."

HANDPRINTS/FOOTPRINTS (Pre-K and up)

Children trace around their hands and feet, noting the differences in size and shape.

You'll Need: construction paper, pencils, crayons, scissors, yarn, fabric scraps, buttons

Here's How: Have the children cut out their traced hand and footprints. Make the word "Footprints" from the cutouts of their feet.

Variation: Trace feet on wallpaper and cut out. Add yarn for hair and button eyes to create "Foot Friends."

Follow-up: Read *Feet* by Catherine Chase.

FEET ARE NEAT (Pre-K and up)

Here is a mini-unit you can try to encourage language development and body awareness.

1st Day

You'll Need: Feet! Feet! Feet!

Here's How: Everyone take off shoes and socks. Let's look at our feet. Where are your toes? Count them. Which one is the biggest? Wiggle your toes. Find a partner and look at his feet. Put your feet up to his. Whose are bigger? Are his feet exactly like yours? Touch each other's feet. Tickle someone's toes.

2nd Day

Take off shoes and socks again. What is the bottom of your foot called? (sole) Where is your *heel*? What are toenails for? Can you feel bones in your foot? Can you find veins? What is inside of veins?

3rd Day

Shoes and socks off again! Lie on your back with feet in the air. What can those feet do? Clap them together. Wiggle them, twist them. Stand up. Walk on tiptoes. Kick.

4th Day

You'll Need: paper, crayons, feet, scissors

Here's How: Have the children trace a friend's foot. Teacher must have his or her foot traced, too. The children enjoy looking for other large feet to trace. Hold an adult's footprint beside a child's. Compare the two.

5th Day

You'll Need: scrap materials, glue, scissors, yesterday's footprints

Here's How: Foot Fellows—Decorate the paper footprints with yarn, ribbon, or material. Make faces on them.

Discusson: Where can feet go?

FOOT FOLLOW-UP

Shoes: Everyone look at one of your shoes. Where is the heel? sole? tongue? How many shoes make a pair? Do your shoes have laces? buckles? straps? Who is wearing sneakers? loafers? boots? sandals?

What other kinds of footwear can you think of? When it rains, we need _____. For snow we need _____.

Bring in samples of footwear in different sizes (slippers, fishing boots, high heels, wooden shoes). Ask, "Who might wear this?"

Show Dad's shoe and a baby shoe. Let the children try to fit their feet into each.

Bring in old socks and a shoe polish brush and polish. Show the children how to polish their shoes.

FOOT PAINTING (Pre-k and up)

It's messy but so much fun—a good outside warm-weather activity!

You'll Need: fingerpaint, mural paper, bucket of soapy water, and towels for clean-up

Here's How: The children may paint their own feet or their friend's feet. Let them walk on the mural paper. Have the bucket ready to step into when they finish. Towel the feet dry.

Variation: Feet Sheet—use an old sheet instead of mural paper.

YOU MUST HAVE BEEN A BEAUTIFUL BABY
(Pre-K and up)

Children discover how they've changed since they were babies.

You'll Need: baby picture from each child and a current picture, baby gift wrapping paper, bows

Here's How: Present each baby picture to the class. Who do you think this could be? Is this baby happy or sad? What is he wearing? Compare the baby to the child's current picture. How has the baby grown? What things are the same? Cover your bulletin board with gift wrap. Allow each child to put his picture on the bulletin board. Talk about the things babies do. What can you do now that you couldn't do when you were a baby? What things do babies need?

CHALK TALKS (Pre-K and up)

You'll Need: colored chalk

Here's How: Use a concrete area of the playground and ask the children to get into groups of two. Each partner traces around his friend's body. The friends tell things that they like about each other and they put the words in a balloon over the head of the drawing.

HAPPY OR SAD? (Pre-K and up)

The children draw pictures to explore their emotions.

You'll Need: a smile and a frown pinned on your bulletin board or door, crayons, drawing paper

Here's How: The children draw pictures of themselves looking happy or sad. They tape their pictures under the appropriate smile or frown and tell why they feel that way.

FEELING INDICATORS (Pre-K and up)

Children express their feelings, values, and thoughts.

You'll Need: A ditto of happy, angry, and sad faces; a ditto of large flowers, and the following:

I am _____

I like _____

I can _____

Sometimes I _____

two colored-paper circles, glue, yarn

Here's How: <u>Faces:</u> Have the children put an X next to the face that represents the way they felt when they came to school. Put an * next to the way they feel now.

<u>Flowers:</u> Draw expressions on the flowers—happy/sad. Tell me when you have felt this way.

Complete the sentences.

<u>Circles:</u> Each child receives two colored circles and glues them together. Punch a hole at the top and add a string to make a necklace. Write "Happy" on one side and "Sad" on the other. Encourage the children to be aware of the feelings of others. The children turn their circles as their feelings change.

DAISIES TELL (Pre-K and up)

Children create a bulletin board and learn about themselves.

You'll Need: large daisies made from contruction paper on the board (five or more)

Here's How: In the center of the flowers, write a question:

    Examples: What makes you special?
                  When do you have fun?
                  What makes you happy? sad?

Read and discuss the questions. Each child chooses a question and dictates a response. Write the child's name and response on the flower petals. Reproduce the daisies on duplicating masters and make copies that the children can take home and share with their families.

MOOD ROCKS (Pre-K and up)

This activity encourages awareness of feelings, both positive and negative.

You'll Need: rocks, markers

Here's How: Ask each child to find a small rock, one that is round and smooth. Wash the rocks and use the markers to put faces on the rocks: a happy face on one side and a sad face on the other. The class keeps their rocks on their desks with the face showing that represents their feelings at the present time. Remind them to turn the rock over when their feelings change. Observe the rocks and ask the children to write on small pieces of paper the reasons for their feelings. Follow up on complaints and unhappy feelings.

SMILE POCKET (Pre-K and up)

Teach the Girl Scout song, "I Have Something in My Pocket" and have the children make the illustrations. (Girl Scout Pocket Songbook, Girl Scouts of the USA, N.Y., N.Y., 1956)

You'll Need: tagboard patterns of gingerbread people, construction paper, fabric, brass fasteners

Here's How: Have the children trace the patterns onto construction paper. Glue on a fabric square for a pocket. Color in the face and clothes. Give each child a 〜 smile cut from construction paper. Place the smile in the pocket. When the child takes the smile out, he uses the brass fastener to place the smile in the right place on the face. The fastener should be placed in the center of the smile so he can turn the smile upside down to make a frown, depending on his feelings.

FEARS

Young children are afraid of different things at certain ages. They need to know that everyone is afraid at some time and that *we* know their fears are very real. The bibliography at the end of this chapter covers many of the fears experienced by children in their early years. Through literature, children often learn to cope with fear and to overcome it. Here is an activity to help children realize that we all share the same fears.

You'll Need: a collection of pictures that show things children often fear (monsters, storms, big dogs, snakes, haunted houses)

Here's How: Talk about each picture. What makes you afraid? What can you do to become less afraid?

The class can draw pictures of their fears and dictate stories to you about them. Be sure you share *your* fears with them. Make use of the books in the bibliography to find other activities.

CHILDREN'S BOOKS

Blume, Judy, *Otherwise Known as Sheila the Great.* N.Y.: Dutton, 1972. (fear of dogs, spiders, ghosts, etc.)

Breinburg, Petronella. *Shawn Goes to School.* N.Y.: Crowell, 1973. (fears at school)

Carrick, Carol and Carrick, Donald. *Sleep Out.* N.Y.: Seabury Press, 1973. (Chris conquers his own fears.)

Gackenback, Dick. *Harry and the Terrible Whatzit.* N.Y.: Seabury Press, 1977. (fear of the unknown)

Hanson, Joan. *I Won't Be Afraid.* N.Y.: Carol Rhoda Books, Inc., 1968.

Hoban, Russell. *Bedtime for Frances.* N.Y.: Harper and Row, 1960. (fear of dark)

Lifton, Judy. *Goodnight, Orange Monster.* N.Y.: Atheneum Press, 1972.

Mayer, Mercer. *There's a Nightmare in My Closet.* N.Y.: Dial Press, Inc., 1968.

Rogers, Fred. *Mister Rogers Talks About.* N.Y.: Platt and Munk, 1974. (fear of moving, school, doctors)

Sendak, Maurice. *Where the Wild Things Are.* N.Y.: Harper and Row, 1963.

Showers, Paul. *A Book of Scary Things.* N.Y.: Doubleday, 1973. (Adults have fears, too!)

Viorst, Judith. *My Mama Says There Aren't Any Zombies, Ghosts, Vampires, Creatures, Demons, Monsters, Fiends, Goblins or Things.* N.Y.: Atheneum Press, 1973.

Watson, Jane Werner. *Sometimes I'm Afraid.* N.Y.: Golden Press, 1971. (Parents can help deal with fears.)

Weber, Bernard. *Ira Sleeps Over.* Boston, Mass.: Houghton Mifflin, 1972.

Bibliography

CHILDREN'S LITERATURE

Adorjan, Carol Madden. *Someone I Know*. N.Y.: Random House Early Bird Books, 1968.

Alexander, Martha. *Nobody Asked Me If I Wanted a Baby Sister*. N.Y.: Dial Press, Inc., 1971.

Aliki. *My Hands*. N.Y.: Crowell, 1962.

_____ *My Five Senses*. N.Y.: Crowell, 1972.

Alpert, Burton. *Mine, Yours, Ours*. Chicago, Ill.: Whitman, 1977.

Ancona, George. *It's a Baby*. N.Y.: Dutton, 1979.

Anglund, Joan Walsh. *A Friend is Someone Who Likes You*. N.Y.: Harcourt, Brace, Jovanovich, 1958.

_____ *Do You Love Someone?* N.Y.: Harcourt, Brace, Jovanovich, 1971.

_____ *Love Is a Special Way of Feeling*. N.Y.: Harcourt, Brace, Jovanovich, 1960.

_____ *Look Out the Window*. N.Y.: Harcourt, 1959.

Babbitt, Natalie. *Something*. N.Y.: Farrar, Straus and Giroux, 1970.

Baer, E. *Wonder of Hands*. N.Y.: Parents' Magazine, 1970.

Barkin, Carol. *I'd Rather Stay Home*. Milwaukee, Wisc.: Raintree Publishers, Ltd., 1975.

_____ *Sometimes I Hate School*. Milwaukee, Wisc.: Raintree Publishers, Ltd.

Behrens, June. *Who Am I?* Chicago, Ill.: Elkgrove Press, Inc., 1968.

_____ *How I Feel*. Chicago, Ill.: Children's Press, 1973.

Beim, Lorraine and Beim, Jerrold. *The Quarreling Book*. N.Y.: Harcourt, Brace, Jovanovich, 1945.

_____ *Two is a Team*. N.Y.: Harcourt, Brace, Jovanovich, 1945.

Bel Geddes, Barbara. *I Like to be Me*. N.Y.: Young Readers Press, 1963.

Bell, Gina. *Who Wants Willy Wells?* Nashville, Tenn.: Abingdon Press, 1965.

Berends, Polly. *Who's That in the Mirror?* N.Y.: Random House, 1968.

Berger, Terry. *I Have Feelings.* Behavioral Publications, Inc., 1971.

Binzen, Bill. *First Day in School.* N.Y.: Coward, McCann and Geoghegan, 1970.

Blume, Judy. *The One in the Middle Is the Green Kangaroo.* Chicago, Ill.: Reilly and Lee, 1969.

_____ *Otherwise Known as Sheila the Great.* N.Y.: Dutton, 1972.

Breinburn, Petronella. *Shawn Goes to School.* N.Y.: Crowell, 1973.

Brenner, Barbara. *Bodies.* N.Y.: Dutton, 1973.

_____ *Faces.* N.Y.: Dutton, 1970.

Brothers, A. and Holsclaw, C. *Just One Me.* Chicago, Ill.: Follet, 1967.

Brown, Myra. *Amy and the New Baby.* N.Y.: Watts, 1965.

_____ *First Night Away from Home.* N.Y.: Watts, 1960.

_____ *Benjy's Blanket.* N.Y.: Watts, 1962.

Buckley, Helen E. *Grandfather and I.* N.Y.: Lathrop, Lee and Shepard Co., Inc., 1969.

_____ *Michael Is Brave.* N.Y.: Lathrop, 1971.

Burton, Virginia Lee. *Mike Mulligan and His Steam Shovel.* Boston, Mass: Houghton Mifflin Co., 1939.

Carrick, Carol and Carrick, Donald. *Sleepout.* N.Y.: Seabury Press, 1973.

Charlip, Remy and Moore, Lillian. *Hooray For Me.* N.Y.: Parents' Magazine, 1975.

Chase, Catherine. *Feet.* N.Y.: Dandelion Press, Inc., 1979.

Child's World Editors. *How Do You Feel?* Elgin, Ill.: Child's World, 1973.

Clark, Ann Nolan. *In My Mother's House.* N.Y.: Viking, 1941.

Clure, Beth and Rumsey, Helen. *Me!* Glendale, Calif.: Bowan Publishing Co., 1968.

Cohen, Miriam. *Will I Have a Friend?* N.Y.: Macmillan, 1967.

Cole, William and Ungerer, Tomi. *Frances Face-Maker—A Going to Bed Book.* N.Y.: World Publishing Co., 1963.

Cretan, Gladys. *Me, Myself and I.* N.Y.: Morrow and Co., 1969.

Darby, Gene. *Like You and Me.* Westchester, Ill.: Benefic Press, 1970.

DeRegniers, Beatrice. *How Joe the Bear and Sam the Mouse Got Together.* N.Y.: Parents' Magazine, 1965.

Dunn, Phoebe and Tris. *Feelings.* Mountain View, Calif.: Creative Education, 1970.

Ets, Marie Hall. *Just Me.* N.Y.: Viking, 1965.

—— *Play With Me.* N.Y.: Viking, 1955.

Fassler, Joan. *The Boy With a Problem.* N.Y.: Human Science Press, 1971.

Fatio, Louise. *Hector Penguin.* N.Y.: McGraw-Hill, 1973.

Feinstein, Joe. *A Silly Little Kid.* Harrisburg, Pa.: Stackpole, 1969.

Feston, Edward. *Fierce John.* N.Y.: Dell, 1974.

Gackenback, Dick. *Harry and the Terrible Whatzit.* N.Y.: Seabury Press, 1977.

Gay, Zhenya. *Who's Afraid?* N.Y.: Viking, 1965.

Golden, Augusta. *Straight Hair, Curly Hair.* N.Y.: Crowell, 1969.

Green, M. M. *Is it Hard? Is it Easy?* N.Y.: Young Scott, 1960.

Hanson, Joan. *I Won't Be Afraid.* N.Y.: Carol Rhoda Books, Inc., 1968.

Hays, Geoffrey. *Bear By Himself.* N.Y.: Harper and Row, 1976.

Hazen, Barbara Shook. *The Me I See.* Nashville, Tenn.: Abingdon Press, 1978.

—— *Happy, Sad, Silly, Mad.* N.Y.: Grossett and Dunlap, 1971.

Hitte, K. *Boy, Was I Mad.* N.Y.: Parents' Magazine Press, 1969.

Hoban, Russell. *Bedtime for Francis.* N.Y.: Harper and Row, 1960.

Horvath, B. *Hooray for Jasper.* N.Y.: Watts, 1966.

Hutchins, Pat. *Titch.* N.Y.: Macmillan, 1971.

Hyde, Margaret and Forsyth, Elizabeth. *Know Your Feelings.* N.Y.: Watts, 1975.

Iwaski, C. *Will You Be My Friend?* N.Y.: McGraw-Hill, 1974.

Jewell, Nancy. *Cheer up Pig.* N.Y.: Harper & Row, 1975.

Johnson, Crockett. *Harold and the Purple Crayon.* N.Y.: Harper & Row, 1958.

Kafka, Sherry. *Big Enough.* N.Y.: Putnam and Sons, 1974.

Kaufmann, Alicia. *Little Is Nice.* N.Y.: Hawthorne, 1970.

Keats, Ezra Jack. *Peter's Chair.* N.Y.: Harper & Row, 1967.

_____ *Dreams.* N.Y.: Macmillan, 1974.

Kessler, E. and L. *Do Baby Bears Sit in Chairs?* N.Y.: Doubleday, 1961.

Kottler, Dorothy and Willis, Eleanor. *I Really Like Myself.* Nashville, Tenn.: Aurora Publications, 1974.

Krasilovsky, Phyllis. *The Shy Little Girl.* N.Y.: Houghton Mifflin, 1970.

Kraus, Robert. *Leo, The Late Bloomer.* N.Y.: Putnam and Sons, 1973.

Krauss, R. *Growing Story.* N.Y.: Harper & Row, 1947.

_____ *Bundle Book.* N.Y.: Harper & Row, 1951. (warm feelings)

Kroll, Steven. *That Makes Me Mad.* N.Y.: Pantheon, 1976.

La Fontaine, Jeanne. *The Lion and the Rat.* N.Y.: Watts, 1963.

Lasker, Joe. *He's My Brother.* N.Y.: Whitman, 1974.

Leaf, Munro. *Boo, Who Used to be Scared of the Dark.* N.Y.: Random House, 1949.

Lenski, L. *Big Little Davy.* N.Y.: Walck, 1956.

LeShan, Eda. *What Makes Me Feel This Way?* N.Y.: Macmillan, 1972.

Lesieg, Thoe. *I Wish I Had Duck Feet.* N.Y.: Random House, 1965.

Lifton, Judy. *Goodnight, Orange Monster.* N.Y.: Atheneum Press, 1972.

Littledale, Harold. *Alexander.* N.Y.: Parents' Magazine, 1964.

Loyal, Nye. *What Color Am I*. Nashville, Tenn.: Abingdon Press, 1977.

Lund, D. *Did You Ever?* N.Y.: Parents' Magazine, 1965. (joy of being)

Mack, Nancy. *Why Me?* Milwaukee, Wisc.: Raintree, Ltd., 1976.

Mahan, Gail. *The Gold of Friendship*. Kansas City, Mo.: Hallmark Cards, Inc., 1958.

Mannheim, G. *Two Friends*. N.Y.: Knopf, 1968.

Mayer, Mercer. *You're the Scaredy Cat*. N.Y.: Parents' Magazine, 1974.

_____ *There's a Nightmare In My Closet*. N.Y.: Dial Press, 1968.

Memling, Carl. *What's in the Dark?* N.Y.: Parents' Magazine, 1971.

Miles, Betty. *Around and Around—Love*. N.Y.: Knopf, 1975.

Moncure, Jane Belk. *About Me*. Chicago, Ill.: Children's Press, 1976.

Moore, Lillian. *Hooray for Me*. N.Y.: Parents' Magazine, 1975.

Ness, E. *Exactly Alike*. N.Y.: Scribner's, 1964.

Piper, Watty. *The Little Engine That Could*. N.Y.: Platt and Munk Publishers

Pollack, Reginald. *The Magician and the Child*. N.Y.: Atheneum, 1971.

Raebeck, L. *Who Am I? Activity Songs for Young Children*. Chicago, Ill.: Follett, 1967.

Rey, Margaret. *Curious George Goes to the Hospital*. N.Y.: Houghton Mifflin, 1966.

Rogers, Fred. *Mister Rogers Talks About*. N.Y.: Platt and Munk, 1974.

Rosenbaum. *What Is Fear?* Englewood Cliffs, N.J.: Prentice-Hall, 1972.

Saroyan, William. *Me*. N.Y.: Crowell-Collier Press, 1963.

Schlein, Miriam. *Billy, The Littlest One*. Chicago, Ill.: Whitman, 1960.

Scott, Ann Herbert. *Sam*. N.Y.: McGraw-Hill, 1967.

Sendak, Maurice. *Where the Wild Things Are.* N.Y.: Harper & Row, 1963.

Sesame Street Book of People and Things. Boston, Mass.: Little, Brown & Co., 1971.

Shick, E. *Making Friends.* N.Y.: Macmillan, 1969.

Showers, Paul. *Your Skin and Mine.* N.Y.: Crowell, 1965.

_____ *A Book of Scary Things.* N.Y.: Doubleday, 1973.

_____ *Follow Your Nose.* N.Y.: Doubleday, 1963.

_____ *Look At Your Eyes.* N.Y.: Doubleday, 1962.

Simon, Nova. *I Know What I Like.* Chicago, Ill.: Whitman, 1971.

_____ *I Was So Mad.* Chicago, Ill.: Whitman, 1974.

_____ *All Kinds of Families.* Chicago, Ill.: Whitman Co., 1975.

_____ *How Do I Feel?* Chicago, Ill.: Whitman Co., 1970.

Slepian, Jan and Seidler, Ann. *An Ear to Hear.* N.Y.: Follett, 1967.

Stanek, Muriel. *I Can Do It.* Westchester, Ill.: Benefic Press, 1967.

_____ *I Won't Go Without a Father.* Racine, Wisc.: Whitman Co., 1972.

Stanley, J. *It's Nice to be Little.* Chicago, Ill.: Rand McNally, 1965.

Stein, Mark. *Good and Bad Feelings.* N.Y.: William Morrow & Co., 1976.

Steptoe, John. *Stevie.* N.Y.: Harper & Row, 1969.

Stevens, Carla. *Hooray for Pig.* N.Y.: Seabury Press, 1974.

Stone, Elbeda. *I'm Glad I'm Me.* N.Y.: Putnam and Sons, 1971.

Udry, Janice May. *What Mary Jo Shared.* Chicago, Ill.: Whitman, 1966.

_____ *Let's be Enemies.* N.Y.: Harper & Row, 1961.

Vasilu, M. *The World is Many Things.* N.Y.: John Day, 1967.

Veen, Mary. *Meredith Was Afraid.* Chicago, Ill.: Children's Press, 1969.

Viorst, Judith. *Alexander and the Terrible, Horrible, No Good, Very Bad Day.* N.Y.: Atheneum, 1976.

_____ *My Mama Says There Aren't Any Zombies, Ghosts, Vampires, Creatures, Demons, Monsters, Fiends, Goblins or Things.* N.Y.: Atheneum, 1973.

Vroman, Tom. *Alexander.* N.Y.: Parents' Magazine, 1964.

Waber, B. *Ira Sleeps Over.* Boston, Mass.: Houghton Mifflin, 1972.

Walley, Dean. *The Book of Me.* Kansas City, Mo.: Hallmark Cards, Inc.,

_____ *I Wish I Could.* Kansas City, Mo.: Hallmark, 1970.

Ward, Lynd. *The Biggest Bear.* N.Y.: Houghton Mifflin, 1952.

Watson, Jane. *Sometimes I Get Angry.* Racine, Wisc.: Golden Press, 1971.

_____ *Sometimes I Get Jealous.* Racine, Wisc.: Golden Press, 1972.

_____ *My Body and How it Works.* Racine, Wisc.: Golden Press, 1972.

Werner, Jane Watson. *Sometimes I'm Afraid.* Racine, Wisc.: Golden Press, 1971.

_____ *Look At Me Now.* Racine, Wisc.: Golden Press, 1971.

Will and Nicolas. *The Little Tiny Rooster.* N.Y.: Harcourt, Brace, Jovanovich, 1960.

Yashima, Taro. *Youngest One.* N.Y.: Viking Press, 1960. (Emotions are common to all.)

_____ *Crow Boy.* N.Y.: Viking Press, 1955. (There is something good in all of us.)

Zolotow, Charlotte. *The Hating Book.*: N.Y.: Harper & Row, 1969.

_____ *Hold My Hand.* N.Y.: Harper & Row, 1972.

_____ *Over and Over.* N.Y.: Harper & Row, 1957.

_____ *William's Doll.* N.Y.: Harper & Row, 1972.

_____ *My Friend John.* N.Y.: Harper & Row, 1968.

_____ *New Friend.* N.Y.: Abelard-Schuman, 1968.

PROFESSIONAL RESOURCES

Branden, Nathaniel. *The Psychology of Self-Esteem*. N.Y.: Bantam, 1969.

Canfield, Jack and Wells, Harold. *100 Ways to Enhance Self-Concept in the Classroom*. Englewood Cliffs, N.J.: Prentice-Hall, Inc., 1976.

Coppersmith, Stanley. *The Antecedents of Self-Esteem*. San Francisco, Calif.: Freeman and Co., 1967.

Cullum, Albert. *The Geranium on the Window Sill Just Died But Teacher You Went Right On*. Holland: Harlin Quist, Inc., 1971.

Dinkmeyer, Don and McKay, Gary D. *Parent's Handbook*. Minn.: American Guidance Service, Inc., Circle Press, 1976.

Dorian, Margery and Gulland, Francis. *Telling Stories Through Movement*. Palo Alto, Calif.: Fearon Publishers, 1974.

Drew, Walter F. and Olds, Anita R. *Motivating Today's Students*. Palo Alto, Calif.: Education Today Co., Inc., 1974.

Kiester, D. J. *Who Am I? The Development of Self-Concept*. (Eric ED082817) Durham, North Carolina: Learning Institute of North Carolina, 1973.

Kokska, Sharon. *Creative Movement for Special Education*. Belmont, Calif.: Lear Siegler, Inc., Fearon Pub., 1974.

Moore, Raymond S. and Dorothy, N. *Better Late Than Early*. N.Y.: Reader's Digest Press, 1975.

Peairs, L. and Peairs, R. H. *What Every Child Needs*. N.Y.: Harper & Row, 1974.

Samuels, Shirley C. *Enhancing Self-Concept in Early Childhood*. N.Y.: Human Sciences Press, 1977.

Stern, C. and Luckenbill, M. *The Study of Self-Concept in Young Children*. An Annotated Bibliography. (Eric ED076246) Washington, D.C.: Office of Economic Opportunity Research No. OED-CC-99 38, 1972.

Thomas, Marlo (introduced by). *Free To Be You and Me*. N.Y.: McGraw-Hill, 1974.

Todd, V.E. and Hefferman, H. *The Years Before School: Guiding the Pre-school Children.* N.Y.: Macmillan, 1970.

Yamamoto, K. *The Child and His Image: Self-Concept in the Early Years.* Boston, Mass.: Houghton-Mifflin, 1972.

FILMS/FILMSTRIPS/PROGRAMS/KITS*

Free To Be You and Me, Part I, (16 min. color), 16mm
"*Friendship and Cooperation*"—*Investigates the two-way street of interpersonal relationships with friends and siblings. Conflicts that may arise and the rewards of love and sharing.*

Free To Be You and Me, Part II, (14 min. color), 16mm
"*Expectations*"—*Examines life-goals and social roles from the point of individual fulfillment, rather than the generalized formulas of acceptability.*

Free To Be You and Me, Part III, (17 min. color), 16mm
"*Independence*"—*Fosters self-reliance by developing the conviction that one's unique feelings and talents are gifts to be used and never hidden.*

Growing, (7 min. color), 16mm (3—up)
A computer-animated film that uses almost abstract but representative images and visual patterns from nature which synchronize with a musical score to describe life and concept of growth. Designed to give children freedom to respond to visual imagery, but will appeal to all ages. No narration. Directed by Gary Bergland. Produced by Encyclopedia Britannica Educational Corp., 1969. (Computers; Experimental Films; Nature; Seasons; Spring)

The Hand That Would Not Open, (7 min. color), 16mm (3—8)
A hand shows a fist all the things that an open hand can do. Shots of people at work and play expand the idea of a hand's versatility. Narration is a song. Produced by Abracadabra Enterprises Corp., 1971. (Children's Stories)

*All films listed here are distributed by McGraw-Hill, 1974.

Just One Me, (9 min. color), 16mm (3—8)

Live action is used in unusual ways to show how an imaginative Negro boy pictures himself as a tree, a road, a merry-go-round, the wind, a plane, etc. He enjoys his many roles, but returns at last to the most unique one—himself. Based on the book by Aileen Brothers and Cora Holsclaw. Folk song accompaniment by Juniper. Directed by Peter Scheer. Produced by Stelios Roccos, 1971. (Black-Americans; Children's Stories)

The Metooshow: If I Were an Animal . . ., (20 min. color), 16mm (3—8, Adult)

When asked during an interview, "If you could be an animal, what would you be, and why?," the children's responses are unexpected and improbable. They find many ways to express the looks and sounds of their favorite animals. Included are a number of craft projects that children and adults can participate in together. Produced by Norman J. Cohn, Three Prong TV Productions, Inc., 1969. (Animals; Arts and Crafts; Child Care and Development; Education)

FILMSTRIPS

"Growing To Know Me," Classroom World Productions, 1975. (Pre-K and Primary)

Includes: "Is There Still Room For Me?"
"A Rainy Day"
"The People Next Door"
"The Special Gift"
"I Think It's Really Broken"

"It's Good To Be Me," Q-Ed Publicatons, 1976. (Primary)

Includes: "Lions and Tigers and Bears"
"Different Is OK"
"Once Upon a Swing"
"Birthday Bike"
"So Big"

"Looking At Yourself," Pathescope Educational Media, Inc., 1977. (Grades 4—8)
 Includes: "Knowing Yourself"
      "Understanding Others"

"Knowing Me/Knowing You," Coronet Instructional Media Co., 1978. (K—3)
 Includes: "The I Feel Game"
      "The You Feel Game"
      "The No Blame Game"
      "I Want You Game"

"Who Am I?," Kindle Series, Inside Out Productions, Inc., for Scholastic, 1972. (Pre-K and Primary)
 Includes: "The Joy of Being You"
      "People Packages"
      "All Kinds of Feelings"
      "Do You Believe in Wishes?"

"You and Your Family Unit," Benefic Press, 1972. (Primary)
 Includes: "You and Your Family"
      "You and Your Friends"
      "You and Others"
      "My Friends and I"
      "I Can Do It"

TEACHING RESOURCES

Moveable Melvin (jointed figure). Webster Division, McGraw-Hill Book Co., Manchester, Missouri, 1972.

Roundabout Teacher Manual, NCSCT, Box A, Bloomington, Ind., 1973.
 Includes: "A Pair Needs Two"
      "Living or Dead"
      "Children Everywhere"
      "What's Inside of Me"

RECORDS

"Feelin' Free," by Hap Palmer. Educational Activities, Inc., 1976.

"Free To Be You and Me," by Marlo Thomas and Friends. Artista Records, Produced by Carole Hart, 1972.

"Getting To Know Myself," by Hap Palmer. Educational Activities, Inc., 1972.

"Good Apple Activities to Improve Self-Concept, The Ballad of Lucy Lum Record and Book," by Joe Wayman and Don Mitchell. Good Apple Inc., 1977.

"Ideas, Thoughts, and Feelings," by Hap Palmer, Educational Activities, Inc., 1973.

"My Street Begins At My House," by Ella Jenkins. Folkways Records and Service Corp., 1971.

"Pretend," by Hap Palmer, Educational Activities, Inc., 1975.

"Sesame Street Every Body's Record," Sesame Street Records Div. of Distinguished Products, Inc., 1979.

"What A Wonderful Thing Is Me," Walt Disney Productions. By Tom and Frances Adair. 1973.

"We All Live Together," by Peggy Brogan and Bill Martir, Youngheart Music, 1978.

SONGS

"Everything Grows Together," by Fred Rogers. *Mister Rogers' Songbook*, N.Y.: Random House, 1970.

"It's Me," by Carmino Ravosa. *Early Years Magazine*, Allen Raymond, Inc., September, 1977.

"It's Such A Good Feeling, To Know You're Alive," by Fred Rogers. *Mister Rogers' Songbook*, N.Y.: Random House, 1970.

"Right in the Middle of My Face," by Jeffrey Moss. *Sesame Street Songbook*, N.Y.: Simon and Schuster, in conjunction with the Children's Television Workshop, 1971.

"Special," by Jeffrey Moss. *Sesame Street Songbook*, Children's Television Workshop, 1971.

"Someone Nice," by Joe Raposo. *Sesame Street Songbook*, Children's Television Workshop, 1977.

POEMS

Bouton, Josephine. *Favorite Poems for the Children's Hour*. N.Y.: Platt and Munk, 1967.

1. "Come Along In, Then, Little Girl," by Edna St. Vincent Millay
2. "My Shadow," by Robert Louis Stevenson
3. "My Feet," by Gelett Burgess
4. "Extremes," by James Whitcomb Riley

Hopkins, Lee Bennett. *Girls Can Too!* N.Y.: Franklin Watts, 1972.

_____ *Poems Children Will Sit Still For*. N.Y.: Scholastic Book Services, 1971.

1. "On Our Way," by Eve Merriam
2. "Big Little Boy," by Eve Merriam
3. "Brother," by Mary Ann Hoberman
4. "Politeness," by A. A. Milne
5. "We Must Be Polite," by Carl Sandburg
6. "8 A.M. Shadows," by Patricia Hubbell

Index

Editor's Note: entries in **boldface** are names of activities